MICHAEL HUTT

INVOKING
THE INCREDIBLE
POWER
OF ALTARS & SACRIFICES

(PROVOKING THE SUPERNATURAL THROUGH ALTARS AND SACRIFICES)

HWP

INVOKING THE INCREDIBLE POWER OF ALTARS AND SACRIFICES

ISBN 978-1-912252-11-4

Published & Distributed by:
Hutton-Wood Publications

In the UK write to:
Michael Hutton-Wood Ministries
1st Floor, 387 London Road, Croydon. CR0 3PB

Or Call:
020 8689 6010 / 079 568 15714

Outside the UK, Call:
+44 20 8689 6010; +44 7956 815 714

Or Contact:
www.houseofjudah.org.uk
michaelhutton-wood.org

E-mail:
michaelhuttonwood@gmail.com
leadersfactoryinternational@yahoo.com

Designed by:
Indes Procom Ltd
+233 264 881 018
www.indesprocom.com

Printed:
In the United Kingdom
HWP

Content

The Mandate

'...Set in order the things that are out of order and raise and appoint leaders in every city.' - Titus 1:5

MICHAEL HUTTON-WOOD MINISTRIES
Releasing Potential
- Maximizing Destiny

HOUSE OF JUDAH (PRAISE) MINISTRIES
& LEADERS FACTORY INTERNATIONAL
Raising Generational Leaders
- Impacting Nations

SIMPA:
SCEPTRE INTERNATIONAL MINISTERS
& PASTORS ASSOCIATION
Equipping, Empowering, Coaching, Mentoring
And Providing Covering For Pastors, Ministers
And Leaders Across The Nations!

Dedication

Dedicated to

The Altars Of Those Who Sacrificed Immensely And Paved The Way And Still Do, For Us To Be Who We Are In Ministry And Leadership Today.

GREATER GRACE!!!

*At the root of
everything outstanding, is
understanding!!!*

Introduction

In this book, we will be revealing the incredible power of this mystery of Altars and Sacrifices which has existed right from Genesis. The first time you hear of offerings, altars and sacrifices is in Genesis as well which shows how important it is in our victorious walk.

At the root of everything outstanding is understanding!

Ignorance is a killer and is the most affordable commodity in the market (Hosea 4:6). They used to say 'What you don't know will not hurt you', but the truth is, what you don't know can kill you.

IGNORANCE IS THE DEADLIEST KILLER ON THIS EARTH, not the AIDS virus. That's why the Psalmist prayed in Psalm 119:144; 'Give me understanding that I might live.'

ALTARS ARE PLACES WHERE DESTINIES ARE DECIDED AND WHAT TRIGGERS ALTARS ARE SACRIFICES, SERVICE, TITHES, OFFERINGS, PRAISE, PRAYER AND PLEADING YOUR CASE WITH THE WORD. Without Sacrifices, the altar remains dormant and inactive. It is sacrifices, tithes and offerings that bring life to altars. It is your offerings and sacrifices that activate your altar and fire from heaven and Fire only comes down in response to sacrifices on altars. There is no way you can expect certain fires from heaven until you've activated your altars through sacrifices, tithes and offerings.

Sacrifices are:

i. The key to the Supernatural Anointing.

ii. The key to Power

iii. The key to Divine Wisdom

iv. The key to God's Presence

v. The key to Divine Prosperity and Wealth

vi. The key to the manifestation of signs, wonders and power

vii. The key to Dramatic Turnarounds

viii. The key to Restoration and Restitution

YOU CANNOT WITHDRAW FROM AN ALTAR YOU HAVE NOT GIVEN TO.

THERE ARE CERTAIN DIMENSIONS OF GOD AND THE SUPERNATURAL YOU AND YOUR CHILDREN CAN NEVER CONTACT UNTIL YOU UNDERSTAND AND ARE ADDICTED TO SACRIFICES. UNDERSTANDING TITHING, SACRIFICES, OFFERINGS AND HOW TO ACTIVATE THE ALTARS OF YOUR CHURCH IS CRUCIAL.

Many give to earthly things more than spiritual things like clubs, society, shopping, clothes, shoes, food and so see only earthly things and meet only men and get only what men can give.

AN ALTAR HOWEVER, IS WHERE YOU GIVE TO GOD TO PROVOKE WHAT'S IN HIS HAND. GOD DOES NOT NEED ANYTHING, SO WHEN WE GIVE TO HIM, WE ARE GIVING TO SOMEONE WHO OWNS EVERYTHING, DOES NOT NEED ANYTHING AND SO, ENTER HIS CLASS WHERE ALL OUR NEEDS ARE MET BECAUSE JUST LIKE HIM WE ALSO DON'T NEED ANYTHING.

YOU DON'T NEED ANYTHING IF YOU HAVE EVERYTHING, DO YOU?

That's God's class and our class and that's why YOU MUST GIVE TO GOD AND TO HIS WORK MORE by laying up treasures in heaven.

In this book, you will also discover the DIFFERENCES BETWEEN A STAGE, PLATFORM and ALTARS, so, you are not confused but adequately informed to take advantage of everything that Altars offer.

1. A stage is where contracts are made; An altar is where covenants are made.

2. A stage is where contracts are signed; An altar is where covenants are sealed.

3. A stage is for physical manifestations; an altar is for supernatural manifestations.

4. A stage is where we present our bodies and gifts to please and entertain men; An altar is where we present our bodies as living sacrifices (Romans 12:1-2).

5. A stage is where performances and acts of men take place; an altar is where supernatural acts of God take place.

6. A stage is where flesh meets flesh; an altar is where spirits meet spirits.

7. A stage is where men meet men; an altar is where God meets men.

8. A stage is where humanity meets humanity; an altar is where divinity meets humanity.

9. A stage is where men entertain men; an altar is where God transforms men.

10. A Stage is where man provokes applause, accolades and recognition; an altar is where you invoke and provoke the power and presence of God.

In all your getting, get understanding and Get ready to engage this mystery so as to gain mastery in every area.

"And they overcame him by the blood of the Lamb, and by the word of their testimony; and they loved not their lives unto the death."

- Revelation 12:11

Chapter One

MY PERSONAL TESTIMONY
ABOUT ALTARS AND SACRIFICES

Psalms 119:129,
*"Thy testimonies are wonderful: therefore doth
my soul keep them."*

Psalms 119:46,
*"I will speak of thy testimonies also before kings,
and will not be ashamed."*

Psalms 119:24,
*"Thy testimonies also are my delight and my
counsellors."*

Years ago, I came across and read this scripture in Genesis
14:22-23,

*"But Abram said to the king of Sodom, "I have lifted my hand
to the Lord, God Most High, Possessor of heaven and earth,
that I would not take a thread or a sandal strap or anything
that is yours, lest you should say, 'I have made Abram rich."*

After reading this scripture, I made a vow that, NO ONE WILL EVER SAY THEY MADE ME RICH AND THAT NO ONE WILL BE ABLE TO FIGURE ME OUT, PREDICT MY MOVEMENTS OR BE ABLE TO EXPLAIN WHY OR HOW I AM BLESSED.

YOU MUST AIM TO BECOME A WONDER! A 'WHAT MANNER OF MAN IS THIS!' A MAN OR WOMAN OR LEADER WHOSE WISDOM MAKES PEOPLE ASK, 'WHAT WISDOM IS THIS?' AND YEARN FOR WHAT YOU HAVE.

When people leave you unceremoniously, they must hear of your speedy and accelerated success and progress and never return to find you at the same spot.

It's a choice and decision you must make to trust God completely.

Among the many things God loves: GOD LOVES TO BE BELIEVED AND TRUSTED AND TO SHARE HIS GLORY IN OUR LIVES, FAMILIES, CAREERS, MINISTRIES, BUSINESSES, CHURCHES AND ORGANISATIONS WITH NO ONE!

I decided, no one will ever have the audacity to control me, manipulate me financially or economically or claim to take the credit for the happenings in my life, except God. I DECIDED TO BE BECOME AND BE KNOWN OR IDENTIFIED AS A GOD-MADE MAN, NOT, A MAD-MADE MAN, because the arm of flesh can fail you at any time. How right I was from experiences I've had over the years including ministry. I decided, begging and borrowing is finally over. I went on a search for Abraham's secret behind his bold declaration and found he walked by Faith and was a dangerous tither, giver, addicted to erecting altars and offering sacrifices, sought God's face, obeyed God promptly, worked hard and smart and was full of wisdom.

I discovered: GOD IS MY SOURCE AND MEN ARE MERE CHANNELS GOD USES TO BLESS ME, BUT THEY ARE NOT MY SOURCE. SO, WHEN MEN LEAVE ME, I DON'T BREAK DOWN OR GIVE UP BECAUSE MY SOURCE IS STILL AVAILABLE AND TOTALLY RELIABLE and MY GIFT (WEALTH-CREATING TOOL) IS INSIDE ME. (Malachi 3:6; Hebrews 13:8)

HE NEVER CHANGES!
HE IS CONSTANT!
NOTHING DESTABILISES HIM!!

Listen: MOST OF US DEPEND TOO MUCH ON MEN BECAUSE, WE SPEND TOO MUCH TIME WITH MEN; THAT'S WHY WE DON'T SEE MUCH OF GOD or what's in God's hand; and that's why we get so easily disappointed. Instead, we must follow hard after GOD HIMSELF because **He reveals His ways, not, just His acts to THOSE WHO FOLLOW HARD AFTER HIM.** (Psalm 103:7; Psalm 63:8)

IF YOU SEEK HIS FACE THROUGH ALTARS AND SACRIFICES, YOU WILL DEFINITELY SEE HIS HAND. Many don't give because they think God is like men who don't fulfil their promises. **The truth is: God is not a promise-keeping God but a covenant-keeping God.**

Listen: Men are not your source; men are channels God uses to bless us but they are not your source. GOD IS and HE HAS MORE THAN ENOUGH. HIS NAME IS EL SHADDAI.

He said in Haggai 2:6-9,
'The silver is mine and the gold is mine.' He owns the silver and gold and the cattle over a thousand hills!"

But the hand and supplies of God are triggered by altars and altars are activated by sacrifices. My altars and altars of those higher than me who know me and whom I learn from and give to, triggers my blessings and supplies via Wisdom and divine ideas. More of my money goes into the kingdom and the ministry and church I am privileged to lead than anywhere else. Over 25% every week. **I do very strange things in secret and so attract very strange blessings.**

I broke the back of poverty in 1989 by starting to tithe GROSS and in 1996 walking on a £50 note, kicking it, sweeping it into a bin to the astonishment of the flock who did not understand what I was doing; that simple act gave me mastery over money. By that faith act, instead of me serving money, it begun to serve me and not dictate to me or my emotions as to whether to give it or not give. At every birthday I give God and place on our church altar 'twice my age offering' to trigger the next double, I give my whole month or 1st weeks' salary to God every January, give 365 seed every 31st night, I tithe and give 20% offerings by direct debit every week, don't give less than a certain figure at every church anniversary, give offerings in multiples in every service every week, give to individuals every week and to my spiritual father and mentors and those in need including the poor.

Why? Because of the Incredible Power Of Altars and Sacrifices I've discovered. Plagues, accidents, pre-mature death, diabolical intentions, schemes and plots against my life, family and ministry, sickness, terminal diseases have miscarried in satanic wombs and incubators, aborted, averted via my sacrifices and taking proper advantage of altars.

SACRIFICES AND ALTARS SPEAK AND WORK BIG TIME!

That's why the Psalmist said boldly in Psalms 93:5,
"Thy testimonies are very sure: holiness becometh thine house, O Lord, for ever."

As a result, MY ALTAR IS KEPT DELIBERATELY ACTIVE, THICK and WET, ALWAYS SPEAKING and ALWAYS DELIVERING. GOD IS ALWAYS SPEAKING, DOWNLOADING and BLESSING ME WITH DIVINE

IDEAS WHICH I ACT ON THROUGH HARD SMART WORK TO SUCCEED BECAUSE OF MY ADDICTION TO ENGAGING THIS MYSTERY OF THE POWER OF ALTARS AND SACRIFICES.

Bishop Oyedepo said: "IT IS FOOLISHNESS TO BE SHAMEFUL OF WHAT IS GAINFUL!!"

Why would you give up on or be shameful of what has always worked for you?

THE JOYFUL ACT OF CONTINUOUS GIVING TO A BLESSED GOD, BLESSED CHURCH, BLESSED MINISTRY AND BLESSED MAN OR WOMAN OF GOD IS A SMART AND WISE WAY OF TRIGGERING THEIR ALTARS, THEIR GOD, 'ANOINTINGS', GRACES AND PROVOKING WHAT THEY PROVOKE because the lesser is always blessed by the greater altars and spiritual personalities He gives to constantly as confirmed in Hebrews 7:7, *"And without all contradiction the less is blessed of the better."*

Remember: Isaiah 10:27,
"And it shall come to pass in that day, that his burden shall be taken away from off thy shoulder, and his yoke from off thy neck, and the yoke shall be destroyed because of the anointing."

When I hear of or come across a man or woman of God or success story whose anointing and graces I admire or need,

I look for them and sow into their personal lives, ministries, churches, organisations and resource materials i.e. their altars, to go higher. Never see a man of God you call your pastor whom God has blessed and anointed with graces you need and not give to him in one way or the other, if possible, monthly. You trigger his Altars to work for you.

The Shunemite woman in 2 Kings 4 ceased the opportunity to bless, feed, serve, minister to and accommodate Elisha and triggered the anointing on Elisha to terminate barrenness in her life permanently. The widow of Zarephath terminated poverty by obeying the commandment of Elijah the prophet to feed him first. Bible testifies in 1 Kings 17:16, *"And the barrel of meal wasted not, neither did the cruse of oil fail, according to the word of the Lord, which he spake by Elijah."*

CONDITIONS FOR DOUBLE PORTION AND DIVINE WISDOM FROM FATHERS AND MENTORS:

Elisha triggered the double portion of the grace and anointing on his master by pouring water on his hands serving him for at least twenty years and waited as instructed to see him go.

2 Kings 3:11,
"But Jehoshaphat said, Is there not here a prophet of the Lord, that we may enquire of the Lord by him? And one of the king of Israel's servants answered and said, Here is Elisha the son of Shaphat, which poured water on the hands of Elijah."

2 Kings 2:9-10,

"And it came to pass, when they were gone over, that Elijah said unto Elisha, Ask what I shall do for thee, before I be taken away from thee. And Elisha said, I pray thee, let a double portion of thy spirit be upon me. And he said, Thou hast asked a hard thing: nevertheless, if thou see me when I am taken from thee, it shall be so unto thee; but if not, it shall not be so."

2 Kings 2:12-15,

"And Elisha saw it, and he cried, My father, my father, the chariot of Israel, and the horsemen thereof. And he saw him no more: and he took hold of his own clothes, and rent them in two pieces. He took up also the mantle of Elijah that fell from him, and went back, and stood by the bank of Jordan; And he took the mantle of Elijah that fell from him, and smote the waters, and said, Where is the Lord God of Elijah? and when he also had smitten the waters, they parted hither and thither: and Elisha went over. And when the sons of the prophets which were to view at Jericho saw him, they said, The spirit of Elijah doth rest on Elisha. And they came to meet him, and bowed themselves to the ground before him."

SO DID JOSHUA, THROUGH UNFLINCHING, LOYAL, DEVOTED SERVICE:

Deuteronomy 34:9,

"And Joshua the son of Nun was full of the spirit of wisdom; for Moses had laid his hands upon him: and the children of

Israel hearkened unto him, and did as the Lord commanded Moses."

Exodus 33:11,
"And the Lord spake unto Moses face to face, as a man speaketh unto his friend. And he turned again into the camp: but his servant Joshua, the son of Nun, a young man, departed not out of the tabernacle."

Numbers 11:28,
"And Joshua the son of Nun, the servant of Moses, one of his young men, answered and said, My lord Moses, forbid them."

UNTIL YOU DO WHAT SOMEONE GENUINELY SUCCESSFUL AND PROSPEROUS HAS DONE AND IS STILL DOING, YOU CAN NEVER SEE WHAT THEY SEE!

UNTIL YOU DO THE SAME, YOU CANNOT SEE THE SAME AND IF YOU DON'T DO THE SAME, YOU MAY SUFFER THE SHAME!!!

May that not be your story!

IF YOU CAN PLACE EVERYTHING YOU HAVE IN GOD'S HAND, AND TRUST HIM, YOU CAN PROVOKE EVERYTHING IN GOD'S HAND.

The little boy with the five loaves of bread and two fish placed his 'school lunch' in Jesus hands and He blessed it and served thousands of people. In return, he went back home with twelve baskets full. This is how you fill your baskets and bank accounts. Be A Sacrificial Giver! NAME IT; GOD Has it!

Stop putting all your money in banks. Put It in God's bank i.e. the kingdom and receive cash multiples through creativity, witty inventions, divine ideas, innovativeness, divine favour, divine health, fruitfulness, divine wisdom and the prospering of the works of your hands.

Tap into the secrets and unspeakable advantages of Altars via Sacrifices in this book to give you COMPETITIVE ADVANTAGE OVER ALL YOUR COMPETITORS IN YOUR FIELD AND OVER EVERY COMPETITION.

AN ALTAR IS A PLACE WHERE HUMANITY MEETS DIVINITY!

AN ALTAR IS A PLACE WHERE THE NATURAL MEETS THE SUPERNATURAL AND BOWS!

AN ALTAR IS A PLACE WHERE MEN'S VOICE PROVOKES, HEARS AND SUBMITS TO GOD'S VOICE!

AN ALTAR IS A PLACE OF DIVINE ENCOUNTERS!

AN ALTAR IS A PLACE WHERE SPIRITS MEET AND ONE OVERTAKES THE OTHER SUCH AS THE SPIRIT

OF POVERTY IS OVERTAKEN BY THE SPIRIT OF PROSPERITY AND THE SPIRIT OF BARRENNESS OVERTAKEN BY THE SPIRIT OF FRUITFULNESS!

AN ALTAR IS ERECTED FOR THE OFFERING OF SACRIFICES TO ACTIVATE THAT ALTAR.

SO: WHEN YOU SEE OR SENSE LOOMING-DANGER OR BEFORE, ERECT AN ALTAR!

Like Gideon, when you see generational poverty and insignificance in your family's history repeated, tear down the family altars responsible and erect a new altar unto God with sacrificial, inconvenient seeds that smoke God out of heaven like Abel, Noah, Abraham, Solomon, David and Elijah did.

There are offerings and there are sacrificial offerings.

There are convenient and inconvenient offerings. They are not the same.

There are BLESSINGS and there are SWORN BLESSINGS!!

You Choose!
UNTIL SOMETHING LEAVES EARTH, NOTHING LEAVES HEAVEN AND UNTIL SOMETHING QUALITATIVE AND QUANTITATIVE LEAVES EARTH, NOTHING QUALITATIVE AND

QUANTITATIVE LEAVES HEAVEN!!

What Leaves Heaven Is Determined By What Leaves Earth. You decide!

When you take a sacrifice to the altar, you invoke and provoke the presence of the spirits or God. (1 Kings 3:4-51)

When you take a sacrifice to the altar, you invoke and provoke the presence of the spirits or the Spirit of God. (1 Kings 3:4-51)
Altars are places where God comes down by Himself as an All Consuming Fire to Consume fire, offerings and sacrifices and shut the mouth of lions. (Daniel 3 & 6)

Until there is a sacrifice on your altar, fire does not come down and prophecies remain unfulfilled.

Altars are triggered by specified sacrifices.

2 Samuel 24:15 says,
"So the Lord sent a pestilence upon Israel from the morning even to the time appointed: and there died of the people from Dan even to Beersheba seventy thousand men."

2 Samuel 24:18,
"And Gad came that day to David, and said unto him, Go up, rear an altar unto the Lord in the threshingfloor of Araunah the Jebusite."

2 Samuel 24:25,

"And David built there an altar unto the Lord, and offered burnt offerings and peace offerings. So the Lord was intreated for the land, and the plague was stayed from Israel."

Start your journey NOW with UNDERSTANDING and TRIGGER THE SUPERNATURAL!!

"If The First Is Blessed,
The Rest Is Blessed!!"

Chapter Two

THE LAW OF FIRST THINGS

Psalms 119:144,

"The righteousness of thy testimonies is everlasting: give me understanding, and I shall live."

Everything Outstanding Begins With Understanding!!

In the scriptures, there is something called the Law of First things, indicating God's priorities.

The First time we hear of offerings in the Bible is in Genesis 4:3-5,

"And in process of time it came to pass, that Cain brought of the fruit of the ground an offering unto the Lord. And Abel, he also brought of the firstlings of his flock and of the fat thereof. And the Lord had respect unto Abel and to his offering: But unto Cain and to his offering he had not respect. And Cain was very wroth, and his countenance fell."

The First time we hear of altars in the Bible is in Genesis 8:20-22, where God instituted the Law of seedtime and harvest:

Genesis 8:20-22,
"And Noah builded an altar unto the Lord; and took of every clean beast, and of every clean fowl, and offered burnt offerings on the altar. And the Lord smelled a sweet savour; and the Lord said in his heart, I will not again curse the ground any more for man's sake; for the imagination of man's heart is evil from his youth; neither will I again smite any more every thing living, as I have done. While the earth remaineth, seedtime and harvest, and cold and heat, and summer and winter, and day and night shall not cease."

The first thing Noah did when he made it with his family through the flood i.e. when he arrived or landed on Mount Ararat after he and his family of eight were spared from being wiped out with everyone on earth was rear an altar.

Genesis 8:20,
"And Noah builded an altar unto the Lord; and took of every clean beast, and of every clean fowl, and offered burnt offerings on the altar."

DOING THE FIRST THING FIRST IS WHAT QUALIFIES YOU FOR THE REST! **In This Kingdom, Nothing Just Happens! Nothing Happens By Chance! Things Happen For A Reason Or Reasons.**

Proverbs 26:2,
"As the bird by wandering, as the swallow by flying, so the curse causeless shall not come."

Exodus 15:26,
"And said, If thou wilt diligently hearken to the voice of Jehovah thy God, and wilt do that which is right in his eyes, and wilt give ear to his commandments, and keep all his statutes, I will put none of the diseases upon thee, which I have put upon the Egyptians: for I am Jehovah that healeth thee."

Exodus 23:25-26,
"And ye shall serve Jehovah your God, and he will bless thy bread, and thy water; and I will take sickness away from the midst of thee. There shall nothing cast their young, nor be barren, in thy land: the number of thy days I will fulfil."

FOOLS BELIEVE IN LUCK, WHILE THE WISE, BELIEVE IN THE LAW OF CAUSE AND EFFECT!!

Isaiah 1:19-20,
"If ye be willing and obedient, ye shall eat the good of the land: But if ye refuse and rebel, ye shall be devoured with the sword: for the mouth of the Lord hath spoken it."

Job 36:11,
"If they obey and serve him, they shall spend their days in prosperity, and their years in pleasures."

God speaking through wisdom personified in Proverbs 8:17-21 said:

"I love them that love me; and those that seek me early shall find me. Riches and honour are with me; yea, durable riches and righteousness. My fruit is better than gold, yea, than fine gold; and my revenue than choice silver. I lead in the way of righteousness, in the midst of the paths of judgment: That I may cause those that love me to inherit substance; and I will fill their treasures."

DOING THE FIRST THING FIRST IS WHAT QUALIFIES YOU FOR THE REST AND REST ON EVERY SIDE!!

1 Kings 5:4,
"But now the Lord my God hath given me rest on every side, so that there is neither adversary nor evil occurrent."

Matthew 6:31-33,
"Therefore take no thought, saying, What shall we eat? or, What shall we drink? or, Wherewithal shall we be clothed? (For after all these things do the Gentiles seek:) for your heavenly Father knoweth that ye have need of all these things. But SEEK YE FIRST the kingdom of God, and his righteousness; (YOUR VERY LIFE ON GOD'S ALTAR AS A LIVING SACRIFICE (Romans 12:1-2) AND ALL THESE THINGS SHALL BE ADDED UNTO YOU."

Proverbs 3:9-10,

*"Honour the Lord with thy substance, and with the FIRSTFRUITS of all thine increase: (ON ALTARS) SO SHALL THY BARNS BE FILLED WITH PLENTY AND THY PRESSES (MIND) SHALL BURST OUT WITH **NEW WINE** (New Ideas, Divine Ideas, Divine Wisdom, Divine Favour, Creativity, Witty Inventions, Innovation For Wealth Creation)"*

(Order My Book on UNDERSTANDING AND RELEASING THE POWER OF FIRSTFRUIT OFFERINGS from www.houseofjudah.org.uk)

I repeat:
YOU CANNOT PUT GOD FIRST AND BE LAST IN LIFE!

2 Chronicles 20:30,
"So the realm of Jehoshaphat was quiet: for his God gave him rest round about."

You Cannot Serve God On Your Own Terms; You Can Only Serve Him On His Terms!!!

BRINGING THE FIRST BRINGS YOU REST IN YOUR FINANCES AND REST ON EVERY SIDE:

Leviticus 23:9-11,
"And the Lord spake unto Moses, saying, Speak unto the

children of Israel, and say unto them, When ye be come into the land which I give unto you, and shall reap the harvest thereof, then ye shall bring a sheaf of the firstfruits of your harvest unto the priest: And he shall wave the sheaf before the Lord, to be accepted for you: on the morrow after the sabbath the priest shall wave it."

Ezekiel 44:30,
"And the first of all the firstfruits of all things, and every oblation of all, of every sort of your oblations, shall be the priest's: ye shall also give unto the priest the first of your dough, that he may cause the blessing to rest in thine house."

Let me break this scripture down so you can fully understand how this works:

i.   And the FIRST OF ALL THE FIRSTFRUITS OF ALL THINGS,

ii. And every oblation (offering) of ALL,

iii. Of EVERY of your oblations, (offerings)

iv. SHALL BE THE PRIEST'S: (given to him to wave it for you and declare it acceptable for you and present on HIS ALTAR to God)

v.   YE SHALL ALSO GIVE THE PRIEST THE FIRST OF YOUR DOUGH (Money)

RESULT/BENEFITS:

THAT HE (THE PRIEST) MAY CAUSE (Command or Release or Allow) THE BLESSING TO REST IN YOUR HOUSE.

Proverbs 10:22 says:
"It Is The BLESSING OF THE LORD, not, just your job or how hard you work That Makes Rich and Wealthy And Adds No Sorrow To it."

So, from giving your first, the Priest commands or causes the BLESSING TO REST (not up and down but to REST in THINE (Your) HOUSE."

We live in a day where people want everything for free including things that are precious. They just want to drive through and become successful overnight and get their deliverance without knowledge; receive their healing, wealth, riches, prosperity, freedom without doing anything. But the truth is, NOTHING OF VALUE IS EVER FREE! There are things you must do first before you see or handle anything meaningful. I received a devotional this morning, which buttresses this point. It is entitled: GET YOUR HANDS DIRTY.

The Apostle Paul said, *"But by the grace of God I am what I am, and His grace toward me was not in vain; but I laboured more abundantly than they all, yet not I, but the grace of God which was with me"*. (1 Corinthians 15:10)

A business consultant decided to carry out some landscaping on his grounds. He contracted it to an extremely knowledgeable horticulturist who holds a doctorate in horticulture. The business consultant was very busy and did a lot of travelling and so wanted the horticulturist to design his garden such that little or no maintenance would be required on his part. He insisted on having automatic sprinklers and other devices that would minimise his personal involvement in the garden.

The horticulturist said to him, "There's one thing you need to deal with before we go any further. If there's no gardener, there's no garden".

Proverbs 28:19 reads:
"He who tills his land will have plenty of bread, But he who follows frivolity will have poverty enough!"

Ongoing spiritual maturity is a product of personal efforts in cherishing and nourishing your Christian life through prayer, fasting, bible study, giving, service, etc.

Without Spiritual Wood i.e. the Word, there is no Spiritual Fire.

Proverbs 26:20,
"Where no wood is, there the fire goeth out: so where there is no talebearer, the strife ceaseth."

There are no short cuts to success.

In 2 Timothy 1:6, Paul said:
"For this reason I remind you to fan into flame the gift of God, which is in you through the laying on of my hands".

God wants us to break forth in every respect and keep growing. He also wants us to continue to maintain the blessings He has given us, i.e. spiritual gifts, our callings, marriages, children and relationships. Things will never work automatically; we have to take responsibility and we have to get our hands dirty.

Do something about that dream, project and idea today. Do something special about your life the rest of this year and you will get unique results in Jesus' Name.

YOU DON'T GROW BIG TO MANAGE WELL; YOU MANAGE WELL TO GROW BIG!

It is Faithfulness with a few that results in managing more.

Matthew 25:20-21,
"And so he that had received five talents came and brought other five talents, saying, Lord, thou deliveredst unto me five talents: behold, I have gained beside them five talents more. His lord said unto him, Well done, thou good and faithful servant: thou hast been faithful over a few things, I will make thee ruler over many things: enter thou into the joy of thy lord."

Colossians 1:29,
"Whereunto I also labour, striving according to his working, which worketh in me mightily."

1 Timothy 4:14-15,
"Neglect not the gift that is in thee, which was given thee by prophecy, with the laying on of the hands of the presbytery. Meditate upon these things; give thyself wholly to them; that thy profiting may appear to all."

> *"Luck may sometimes help; work always helps".*
> **– Teen Esteem**

> *"Men's natures are alike; it is their habits that separate them."* **– Confucius**

> *"We are what we repeatedly do. Excellence then, is not an act, but a habit."* **– Aristotle**

Powerful! I repeat: **Nothing of value is free; there is a cost and a required price to pay to get it**.

Writing this book came at a joyful, painful, man-hours cost of prayer, focus, desire, dedication, determination, decisiveness, reading, research, thinking, planning, sitting down, writing, correcting, rewriting, time, energy, sacrifice, resources, etc.

FOOLISH PEOPLE BELIEVE IN LUCK; WISE PEOPLE BELIEVE IN THE LAW OF CAUSE AND EFFECT.

Aliko Dangote, Africa's richest man, billionaire with a net worth of $16.7 billion, the owner of the Dangote group, which has interests in commodities said this: *"I built a conglomerate and emerged the richest black man in the world in 2008 but it didn't happen overnight. It took me 30 years to get to where I am today. Youths of today aspire to be like me but they want to achieve it overnight. It's not going to work. To build a successful business, you must start small and dream big. In the journey of entrepreneurship, tenacity of purpose is supreme."*

What separates the rich from the poor is what separates risk-takers from non risk-takers. It's the same reason the rich are getting richer and the poor are getting poorer.

Mike Murdock said humorously: 'Your hatred of the rich may explain your poverty.' (why you are poor)

People's hatred of achievers and risk takers and their habits may explain their stagnation and non-achievement and inability to take risks.

I Repeat:
> *"Men's natures are alike; it is their habits that separate them."* – **Confucius**

*"We are what we repeatedly do. Excellence then,
is not an act, but a habit." – **Aristotle***

Risk-takers adopt good habits they live by daily. Certain people's hatred of the rich may explain their poverty and certain people's hatred of achievers may explain their non-achievement and stagnation in life!!

Luke 4:25-27, [Berean Study Bible]
"But I tell you truthfully that there were many widows in Israel in the time of Elijah, when the sky was shut for three and a half years and great famine swept over all the land. Yet Elijah was not sent to any of them, but to the widow of Zarephath in Sidon. And there were many lepers in Israel in the time of Elisha the prophet. Yet not one of them was cleansed—only Naaman the Syrian."

Unto none was Elijah sent but unto the Widow of Zarephath. Why? God knew that after her initial reluctance, she would obey the principle of giving the first.

The Instruction was: MAKE ME FIRST: The widow had to make Elijah, the prophet, a meal first before she and her son ate any, then and only then was shortage, lack, insufficiency and poverty eliminated from her life permanently.

1 Kings 17:13,
"And Elijah said unto her, Fear not; go and do as thou hast said: but make me thereof a little cake first, and bring it unto me, and after make for thee and for thy son."

Her Latter End Became Far Better Than Her Beginning:

1 Kings 17:15-16,
"And she went and did according to the saying of Elijah: and she, and he, and her house, did eat many days. And the barrel of meal wasted not, neither did the cruse of oil fail, according to the word of the Lord, which he spake by Elijah."

All Prophets Owe You Are Prophetic Instructions For Your Total Deliverance and Freedom:

John 2:5,
"His mother saith unto the servants, Whatsoever he saith unto you, do it."

2 Kings 5:10,
"And Elisha sent a messenger unto him, saying, Go and wash in Jordan seven times, and thy flesh shall come again to thee, and thou shalt be clean."

General 'Big Shot' Naaman: You can be angry all you want; if you want to be healed of your leprosy or for it to disappear permanently, then, go wash in the Jordan. You don't need to see the prophet face to face. Just obey instructions.

John 9:7,
"And said unto him, Go, wash in the pool of Siloam, (which is by interpretation, Sent.) He went his way therefore, and washed, and came seeing."

Exodus 7:19,
"And the Lord spake unto Moses, Say unto Aaron, Take thy rod, and stretch out thine hand upon the waters of Egypt, upon their streams, upon their rivers, and upon their ponds, and upon all their pools of water, that they may become blood; and that there may be blood throughout all the land of Egypt, both in vessels of wood, and in vessels of stone."

Exodus 14:15-16,
"And the Lord said unto Moses, Wherefore criest thou unto me? speak unto the children of Israel, that they go forward: But lift thou up thy rod, and stretch out thine hand over the sea, and divide it: and the children of Israel shall go on dry ground through the midst of the sea."

2 Kings 4:3-4,
"Then he said, Go, borrow thee vessels abroad of all thy neighbours, even empty vessels; borrow not a few. And when thou art come in, thou shalt shut the door upon thee and upon thy sons, and shalt pour out into all those vessels, and thou shalt set aside that which is full."

Proverbs 3:9-10,

"Honour the Lord with thy substance, and with the firstfruits of all thine increase: So shall thy barns be filled with plenty, and thy presses shall burst out with new wine."

Malachi 3:8-12,

"Will a man rob God? Yet ye have robbed me. But ye say, Wherein have we robbed thee? In tithes and offerings. Ye are cursed with a curse: for ye have robbed me, even this whole nation. Bring ye all the tithes into the storehouse, that there may be meat in mine house, and prove me now herewith, saith the Lord of hosts, if I will not open you the windows of heaven, and pour you out a blessing, that there shall not be room enough to receive it. And I will rebuke the devourer for your sakes, and he shall not destroy the fruits of your ground; neither shall your vine cast her fruit before the time in the field, saith the Lord of hosts. And all nations shall call you blessed: for ye shall be a delightsome land, saith the Lord of hosts."

Prophets are usually sent with prophetic instructions to take offerings from you for a prophetic purpose, e.g. you make a room for them, they make prophetic pronunciations and when they lie and wake up, you become pregnant as we saw clearly in 2 Kings 4:16-17,

"And he said, About this season, according to the time of life, thou shalt embrace a son. And she said, Nay, my lord, thou man of God, do not lie unto thine handmaid. And the

woman conceived, and bare a son at that season that Elisha had said unto her, according to the time of life."

2 Chronicles 20:20,
"And they rose early in the morning, and went forth into the wilderness of Tekoa: and as they went forth, Jehoshaphat stood and said, Hear me, O Judah, and ye inhabitants of Jerusalem; Believe in the Lord your God, so shall ye be established; believe his prophets, so shall ye prosper."

Nothing meaningful ever happens by chance. It happens by choice.

Both spiritual and physical (career, professional, business, mental, marital and family) success is never by chance but by choice. Success is not by chance, neither, is prosperity or wealth. Only deep people in God see the deep things of God because, deep calleth unto deep.

Psalms 119:18,
"Open thou mine eyes, that I may behold wondrous things out of thy law."

Psalms 42:7,
"Deep calleth unto deep at the noise of thy waterspouts: all thy waves and thy billows are gone over me."

YOU DON'T CATCH BIG FISH IN SHALLOW WATERS!!!

Psalms 107:23-24,

"They that go down to the sea in ships, that do business in great waters; These see the works of the Lord, and his wonders in the deep."

IT IS ONLY THOSE WHO GO DEEPER IN GOD AND THE THINGS OF GOD, WHO CAN DO BIG BUSINESS WITH GOD AND SEE OR EXPERIENCE THE DEEPER THINGS OF GOD!! It does not come cheap. Your life must be laid on the altar of sacrifice.

Daniel 11:32,

"And such as do wickedly against the covenant shall he corrupt by flatteries: but the people that do know their God shall be strong, and do exploits."

ONLY THOSE ON A QUEST TO KNOW GOD, CAN DO EXPLOITS!!

Psalms 62:5,

"My soul, wait thou only upon God; for my expectation is from him."

Psalms 63:1-2 (A Psalm of David, when he was in the wilderness of Judah),

"O God, thou art my God; early will I seek thee: my soul thirsteth for thee, my flesh longeth for thee in a dry and thirsty land, where no water is; To see thy power and thy glory, so as I have seen thee in the sanctuary."

Psalms 63:8,
"My soul followeth hard after thee: thy right hand upholdeth me."

Psalms 103:7,
"He made known his ways unto Moses, his acts unto the children of Israel."

You cannot discover new lands until you've left your present shores to do deep sea fishing!!

Daniel said in Daniel 9:2,
'... I understood by books ...'

I understood by books, not, by idleness.

AT THE ROOT OF EVERYTHING OUTSTANDING, IS UNDERSTANDING!

God does not cast His pearls before swine and God does not share His secrets with people who are disrespectful of his protocol and people who are not serious. In this Kingdom, people become blessed for a reason and others stay in toiling mode equally for a definite reason.

Luke 5:5-8,
"And Simon answering said unto him, Master, we have toiled all the night, and have taken nothing: nevertheless at thy word I will let down the net. And when they had this

done, they inclosed a great multitude of fishes: and their net brake. And they beckoned unto their partners, which were in the other ship, that they should come and help them. And they came, and filled both the ships, so that they began to sink. When Simon Peter saw it, he fell down at Jesus' knees, saying, Depart from me; for I am a sinful man, O Lord."

THE TOILING ONLY CEASES WITH AN UNDERSTANDING AND APPLICATION OF WHAT YOU'VE UNDERSTOOD!!

That's why King Solomon said: Proverbs 4:7-9,
"Wisdom is the principal thing; therefore get wisdom: and with all thy getting get understanding. Exalt her, and she shall promote thee: she shall bring thee to honour, when thou dost embrace her. She shall give to thine head an ornament of grace: a crown of glory shall she deliver to thee."

IN THIS WORLD, WEALTH IS AN ACQUISITION BUT IN THIS KINGDOM, WEALTH IS AN ENTRUSTMENT! THAT IS, IN THIS WORLD, WEALTH IS ACQUIRED BUT IN THIS KINGDOM, WEALTH IS ENTRUSTED.

You don't catch big fish In shallow waters! People's casual approach to life is the reason most of them become and remain casualties in life.

People's casual approach and lack of understanding of altars, offerings, seed-sowing, tithing, first fruits, protocol, spiritual authority and protocols of churches and pastors is the reason they become casualties in life even after tithing, giving, serving, going to very good churches and having very exceptional and selfless people-minded, people's welfare and wellbeing-seeking pastors, i.e. if they do.

A. YOUR APPROACH TO CHURCH AND ALTARS:

Your Approach To Church and Altars Matters:
Being unaware of where you are, the potential there, who is there, can be highly detrimental to you.

Obadiah 1:17,
"But upon mount Zion shall be deliverance, and there shall be holiness; and the house of Jacob shall possess their possessions."

Genesis 28:16-18,
"And Jacob awaked out of his sleep, and he said, Surely the Lord is in this place; and I knew it not. And he was afraid, and said, How dreadful is this place! This is none other but the house of God, and this is the gate of heaven. And Jacob rose up early in the morning, and took the stone that he had put for his pillows, and set it up for a pillar, and poured oil upon the top of it."

Jacob was right in the presence of God but knew it not. But, the moment he realised it and how sacred and powerful the place was and changed his perception and approach, he built an altar unto God, poured oil and made a vow unto God that changed his life forever.

What Is In Church?

Hebrews 12:18, 22-25,

"For ye are not come unto the mount that might be touched, and that burned with fire, nor unto blackness, and darkness, and tempest,...But ye are come unto mount Sion, and unto the city of the living God, the heavenly Jerusalem, and to an innumerable company of angels, To the general assembly and church of the firstborn, which are written in heaven, and to God the Judge of all, and to the spirits of just men made perfect, And to Jesus the mediator of the new covenant, and to the blood of sprinkling, that speaketh better things than that of Abel. See that ye refuse not him that speaketh. For if they escaped not who refused him that spake on earth, much more shall not we escape, if we turn away from him that speaketh from heaven:"

You can either see it as a social club, entertainment centre, full of hypocrites, an optional place to go or the city of the living God, gate of heaven as Jacob said, with an innumerable company of angels ready to serve you, minister or run errands for you, bring you heavenly packages and healing, wisdom, prosperity and deliverance thorough downloaded answers.

HOW YOU SEE CHURCH, WHAT YOU KNOW AND UNDERSTAND OF CHURCHES, GOD'S SERVANTS and INSTRUCTIONS THEY GIVE YOU WHICH YOU BELIEVE AND OBEY IS WHAT DETERMINES WHAT YOU TAKE FROM CHURCH.

There's not one single miracle in the Bible that was not preceded by instructions. Not one.

Examples: Stretch the rod (Exodus 7:19), sit them down in fifties (Luke 9:14), rear an altar (2 Samuel 24:18), what do you have in your house? (2 Kings 4:1-7), arise and walk (Mark 2:11, 'I say unto thee, Arise, and take up thy bed, and go thy way into thine house.')

If dead bodies like Lazarus' body (John 11), the Damsel (Mark 5:39-42) and the boy at the city of Nain (Luke 7:11-15) could hear the voice of Jesus and come out of the grave, what are you waiting for to come out of that chronic situation and dilemma?

Change your approach to your church, pastors, ministers, leaders, tithes, offerings, service, prayer meetings and sacrifices and you will experience the power of God, the outstretched hand of God on your life and the finger of God in the camp of your enemies and haters.

Listen: IT'S NOT HOW LONG YOU'VE BEEN IN CHURCH THAT COUNTS; IT'S HOW HEART-TIED,

HEART-BONDED, HEART-CONNECTED YOU ARE WITH YOUR SPIRIT, SOUL (MIND, WILL, EMOTIONS) AND BODY.

Stop making excuses and instead, change your perspective and approach!

B. APPROACH TO SERVANTS OF GOD AND THEIR INSTRUCTIONS:

Your Approach To A Servant Of God Makes All The Difference:

2 Chronicles 20:20,
"And they rose early in the morning, and went forth into the wilderness of Tekoa: and as they went forth, Jehoshaphat stood and said, Hear me, O Judah, and ye inhabitants of Jerusalem; Believe in the Lord your God, so shall ye be established; believe his prophets, so shall ye prosper."

Matthew 10:40-41,
"He that receiveth you receiveth me, and he that receiveth me receiveth him that sent me. He that receiveth a prophet in the name of a prophet shall receive a prophet's reward; and he that receiveth a righteous man in the name of a righteous man shall receive a righteous man's reward."

Hosea 12:10,

"I have also spoken by the prophets, and I have multiplied visions, and used similitudes, by the ministry of the prophets."

Hosea 12:13,

"And by a prophet the Lord brought Israel out of Egypt, and by a prophet was he preserved."

Amos 3:7,

"Surely the Lord God will do nothing, but he revealeth his secret unto his servants the prophets."

Ephesians 6:1-3,

"Children, obey your parents in the Lord: for this is right. Honour thy father and mother; (which is the first commandment with promise;) That it may be well with thee, and thou mayest live long on the earth."

2 Kings 4:8-9,

"And it fell on a day, that Elisha passed to Shunem, where was a great woman; and she constrained him to eat bread. And so it was, that as oft as he passed by, he turned in thither to eat bread. And she said unto her husband, Behold now, I perceive that this is an holy man of God, which passeth by us continually."

Psalms 74:9,
"We see not our signs: there is no more any prophet: neither is there among us any that knoweth how long."

They did not see their signs because they did not have or recognise or honour their prophets. Meanwhile, Bible exhorts in that same Psalm:

Psalms 74:20,
"Have respect unto the covenant: for the dark places of the earth are full of the habitations of cruelty."

Give Honour Where Honour Is Due:

1 Thessalonians 5:12-13,
"And we beseech you, brethren, to know them which labour among you, and are over you in the Lord, and admonish you; And to esteem them very highly in love for their work's sake. And be at peace among yourselves."

We Can Do Nothing Against The Truth, But, For The Truth:

2 Corinthians 13:8,
"For we can do nothing against the truth, but for the truth."

The Scriptures Cannot Be Broken:

John 10:35,
"If he called them gods, unto whom the word of God came, and the scripture cannot be broken;"

REMOVE NOT THE ANCIENT LANDMARKS THAT THE FATHERS HAVE SET; BE DILIGENT AT EXECUTING THEM!!! By SO DOING, YOU WILL END UP STANDING BEFORE NOBLES!!

Proverbs 22:28-29,
"Remove not the ancient landmark, which thy fathers have set. Seest thou a man diligent in his business? He shall stand before kings; he shall not stand before mean men."

No matter how upset anyone becomes about the word, his word is settled in heaven and abides forever.

Psalms 119:89-90,
"For ever, O Lord, thy word is settled in heaven. Thy faithfulness is unto all generations: thou hast established the earth, and it abideth."

PERCEPTION DETERMINES APPROACH AND APPROACH DETERMINES YOUR TAKES!!!

All these people received the promises or didn't, based on how they perceived the man of God and the words from the lips of the man of God.

THE ONLY THING A PROPHET OR PASTOR OWES YOU ARE INSTRUCTIONS!

What you don't respect, you don't attract. It is very clear, that Spiritual Understanding is what distinguishes one believer from another. That's why the Psalmist said in Psalm 119:144, '...give me understanding and I shall live.'

Proverbs 21:16,
"The man that wandereth out of the way of understanding shall remain in the congregation of the dead."

From these two scriptures, we see clearly that understanding keeps one alive and among the living, but, lack of understanding kills people and keeps them in the congregation of the dead i.e. Dead people.

GIVE ME UNDERSTANDING THAT I SHALL LIVE! People's casual approach to spiritual things is the reason they become spiritually molested and remain spiritual and physical casualties in life. People's casual and laxadoxical or lackadaisical approach to spiritual things like church, tithing, giving, sacrifices, altars, punctuality, the scriptures, serving in God's house, men and women of God is the reason they keep toiling and living beneath their true status. Understanding distinguishes people and makes them outstanding while laxity, lethargy, apathy, lackadaisical attitudes, ignorance and stubbornness, steals, destroys and kills people including some Christians.

Hosea 4:6,
"My people are destroyed for lack of knowledge: because thou hast rejected knowledge, I will also reject thee, that thou shalt be no priest to me: seeing thou hast forgotten the law of thy God, I will also forget thy children."

The devil takes advantage of people's ignorance, stubbornness, laziness, laxity, apathy, over familiarity with church, pastors and spiritual things, to steal from them, kill them and destroy them as his job description is, as stated clearly in John 10:10,

"The thief cometh not, but for to steal, and to kill, and to destroy: I am come that they might have life, and that they might have it more abundantly."

The word lackadaisical:
The Oxford Dictionaries defines it as Lacking enthusiasm and determination; carelessly, lazy: the adjective says, not giving sufficient attention or thought to avoiding

harm or errors, inattentive, incautious, negligent, remiss; not careful, attentive, meticulous, judicious caused by a lack of attention, not concerned or worried about, careless of one's own safety, showing no interest or effort, casual, giving a careless shrug...

Synonyms: unstudied, artless, casual, effortless, unconcerned, nonchalant, insouciant, languid, leisurely, informal; informal couldn't-care-less attitude.

This attitude is the reason, many don't experience God's maximum or ultimate of 2 Chronicles 25:9b, *'And the man of God answered, The Lord is able to give thee much more than this GOD can give you much more than this...'* i.e., where you are or what you have now.

C. APPROACH TO ALTARS AND SACRIFICES:

NOTICE, HOW CAREFUL NOAH WAS IN BUILDING, THE SELECTION OF HOW AND WHAT TO BRING TO GOD AS AN OFFERING.

Genesis 8:20-22,
"And Noah builded an altar unto the Lord; and took of every clean beast, and of every clean fowl, and offered burnt offerings on the altar."

It's not how long you've done a thing that matters, but, how right and how well you do it. When you don't understand this subject we are about to deal with extensively, you toil through life and suffer avoidable mishaps needlessly.

"And Noah builded an altar unto the Lord; and TOOK OF EVERY CLEAN BEAST, AND OF EVERY CLEAN FOWL, and offered BURNT offerings on the altar"

He was not careless or haphazard about it, but very careful and intentional. Why? GOD IS VERY PARTICULAR ABOUT WHAT, WHY, HOW, WHEN, AND WHERE WE BRING HIS OFFERINGS AND OUR SACRIFICES AND WHO DOES, AS HE WARNED STERNLY IN Malachi 1:6-14,

"A son honoureth his father, and a servant his master: if then I be a father, where is mine honour? and if I be a master, where is my fear? saith the Lord of hosts unto you, O priests, that despise my name. And ye say, Wherein have we despised thy name? Ye offer polluted bread upon mine altar; and ye say, Wherein have we polluted thee? In that ye say, The table of the Lord is contemptible. And if ye offer the blind for sacrifice, is it not evil? and if ye offer the lame and sick, is it not evil? offer it now unto thy governor; will he be pleased with thee, or accept thy person? saith the Lord of hosts. And now, I pray you, beseech God that he will be gracious unto us: this hath been by your means: will he regard your persons? saith the Lord of hosts. Who is there

even among you that would shut the doors for nought? neither do ye kindle fire on mine altar for nought. I have no pleasure in you, saith the Lord of hosts, neither will I accept an offering at your hand. For from the rising of the sun even unto the going down of the same my name shall be great among the Gentiles; and in every place incense shall be offered unto my name, and a pure offering: for my name shall be great among the heathen, saith the Lord of hosts. But ye have profaned it, in that ye say, The table of the Lord is polluted; and the fruit thereof, even his meat, is contemptible. Ye said also, Behold, what a weariness is it! and ye have snuffed at it, saith the Lord of hosts; and ye brought that which was torn, and the lame, and the sick; thus ye brought an offering: should I accept this of your hand? saith the Lord. But cursed be the deceiver, which hath in his flock a male, and voweth, and sacrificeth unto the Lord a corrupt thing: for I am a great King, saith the Lord of hosts, and my name is dreadful among the heathen."

As a result of Noah's careful presentation, Bible says the RESULT was: And the LORD SMELLED A SWEET SAVOUR.

Listen: What Leaves Earth Determines What Leaves Heaven and The Quality and Quantity of What Leaves Earth, Determines The Quality And Quantity Of What Leaves Heaven To You.

Response from Heaven: and the LORD SAID IN HIS HEART, I will not again curse the ground any more for man's sake; for the imagination of man's heart is evil from his youth; neither will I again smite any more every thing living, as I have done. (Trans-generational) While the earth remaineth, seedtime and harvest, and cold and heat, and summer and winter, and day and night shall not cease."

This was followed by the BLESSING in Genesis 9:1-2, *"And God blessed Noah and his sons, and said unto them, Be fruitful, and multiply, and replenish the earth. And the fear of you and the dread of you shall be upon every beast of the earth, and upon every fowl of the air, upon all that moveth upon the earth, and upon all the fishes of the sea; into your hand are they delivered."*

One man's honourable and sacrificial seed-sowing on an altar resulted in God, promising not to flood the whole earth ever again. WHERE IS YOUR ALTAR OF SACRIFICE?

"YOUR GIVING DOES NOT ADD ANYTHING TO GOD BUT, IT ADDS EVERYTHING TO YOU!"

Chapter Three

25 INCREDIBLE TRUTHS
ABOUT ALTARS

1. The altar you service is the altar that services you.

2. The altar you protect is the altar that protects you.

3. The altar you defend is the altar that defends you - Psalm 20:1-3.

4. The altar you give to is the altar that gives back to you - Luke 6:38.

5. The altar you build is the altar that builds you.

6. The altar you repair is the altar that repairs all that needs repairing in you.

7. The altar you maintain is the altar that maintains you.

8. The altar you promote is the altar that promotes you.

9. The altar you fight for is the altar that fights for you.

10. The altar you feed is the altar that feeds you.

11. The altar you provide for is the altar that provides for you.

Malachi 3:10,
"Bring ye all the tithes into the storehouse, that there may be MEAT in MINE HOUSE (Church)? mine house, and prove me now herewith, saith the Lord of hosts, if I will not open you the windows of heaven, and pour you out a blessing, that there shall not be room enough to receive."

YOU ARE NOT HELPING GOD BY TITHING AND GIVING AND SERVICING YOUR ALTAR; YOU ARE HELPING TO PUT AND KEEP FOOD ON YOUR TABLE AND THAT OF YOUR CHILDREN'S CHILDREN BY SERVICING GOD'S ALTAR WHERE YOU EAT FROM EVERY WEEK.

Psalms 119:144b,
'The righteousness of thy testimonies is everlasting: give me understanding, and I shall live.'

12. The altar you put food on is the altar that puts food on your table.

13. The altar you place your offerings on is the altar that offers to announce and recommend your gifts, talents, skills and services for others to buy. (Proverbs 18:16; 17:8; 2 Kings 4)

14. The altar you put money on is the altar that puts money in your hands.

15. The altar you value is the altar that adds value to you, brings you value in life and makes you invaluable in life.

16. The altar you believe in and your attitude towards God's altars you believe in, determines your altitude in life.

17. Your faithfulness (continuity) in fulfilling your obligations towards God's altar in your church determines the fulfilment of God's obligations to you. (Matthew 6:33; Luke 6:38)

18. The altar you pray on is the altar that keeps the preys away. You are either praying or becoming a prey.

In the kingdom, nothing comes free except salvation and even with that, you must confess with your mouth and believe with your heart to receive it. (Romans 10:9-10) When what matters to God or concerns God matters to you and concerns you, what matters to you or concerns you will matter to God and concern God. What you sow is what you reap (Galatians 6:6-10; Genesis 8:20-22; Luke 6:38; Psalm 126; 2 Corinthians 9:6-8).

19. The altar you respect and honour is the altar that respects and honours you. (Proverbs 3:9-10)

20. The altar you elevate is the altar that elevates you.

21. The altar you service is the altar that services you.

PROTOCOL FOR GIVING:

Not all offerings on altars are acceptable to God and that's why God rejected Cain's offering but accepted Abel's in Genesis 4:3-7.

THERE IS A DUE PROTOCOL TO BRINGING TITHES, OFFERINGS, SACRIFICES and PRAYER TO GOD ON ALTARS. WHAT TO BRING, HOW, WHERE, WHEN, WHAT and WHO TO BRING IT TO.

BECAUSE, THERE ARE APPOINTED PLACES AND APPOINTED PRIESTS WHO ARE OR HAVE BEEN SPECIFICALLY CHOSEN TO SERVICE EVERY ALTAR AND WHAT THEY DECREE FROM THOSE ALTARS, IS WHAT HAPPENS according to these two scriptures:

Deuteronomy 12:13-14,
"Take heed to thyself that thou offer not thy burnt offerings in every place that thou seest: But in the place which the Lord shall choose in one of thy tribes, there thou shalt offer thy burnt offerings, and there thou shalt do all that I command thee."

Isaiah 44:24-27,
"Thus saith the Lord, thy redeemer, and he that formed thee from the womb, I am the Lord that maketh all things; that stretcheth forth the heavens alone; that spreadeth abroad the earth by myself; That frustrateth the tokens of the liars, and maketh diviners mad; that turneth wise men backward, and maketh their knowledge foolish; That

confirmeth the word of his servant, and performeth the counsel of his messengers; that saith to Jerusalem, Thou shalt be inhabited; and to the cities of Judah, Ye shall be built, and I will raise up the decayed places thereof: That saith to the deep, Be dry, and I will dry up thy rivers:"

That's why the Psalmist prayed,
"...GIVE ME UNDERSTANDING (AND) THAT I SHALL LIVE." - Psalm 119:144

An Understanding or a lack of understanding of Altars are the difference between poverty and prosperity, success and failure, curses and blessings and those who operate under the influence of humanity or divinity or both. (Judges 6)

HOW YOU GIVE IS AS IMPORTANT AS WHAT YOU GIVE:

God was so angry at his priests for breaking due protocol and bringing polluted, undignified offerings to Him, recorded below, and we are all New Testament priests.

Malachi 1:6-14,
"A son honoureth his father, and a servant his master: if then I be a father, where is mine honour? and if I be a master, where is my fear? saith the Lord of hosts unto you, O priests, that despise my name. And ye say, Wherein have we despised thy name? Ye offer polluted bread upon mine altar; and ye say, Wherein have we polluted thee? In that ye say, The table of the Lord is contemptible. And if ye offer

the blind for sacrifice, is it not evil? and if ye offer the lame and sick, is it not evil? offer it now unto thy governor; will he be pleased with thee, OR ACCEPT THY PERSON? saith the Lord of hosts. And now, I pray you, beseech God that he will be gracious unto us: this hath been by your means: will he regard your persons? saith the Lord of hosts. Who is there even among you that would shut the doors for nought? neither do ye kindle fire on mine altar for nought. I HAVE NO PLEASURE IN YOU, saith the Lord of hosts, NEITHER WILL I ACCEPT AN OFFERING AT YOUR HAND. For from the rising of the sun even unto the going down of the same my name shall be great among the Gentiles; and in every place INCENSE shall be offered unto my name, and a PURE offering: for my name shall be great among the heathen, saith the Lord of hosts. But ye have profaned it, in that ye say, The table of the Lord is polluted; and the fruit thereof, even his meat, is contemptible. Ye said also, Behold, what a weariness is it! (HOW TIRING AND OVERBEARING IT IS TO GIVE) and ye have snuffed at it, saith the Lord of hosts; and ye brought that which was torn, and the lame, and the sick; thus ye brought an offering: SHOULD I ACCEPT THIS OF YOUR HAND? saith the Lord. BUT CURSED BE THE DECEIVER (deceitful) WHICH HATH IN HIS FLOCK A MALE (the best producer), AND VOWETH AND SACRIFICETH UNTO THE LORD A CORRUPT THING, FOR I AM A GREAT KING (Be mindful of who you are giving to for I am a great King, (MENTALITY OF GIVING TO A KING) saith the Lord of hosts, and my name is dreadful (to be FEARED) among the heathen."

FACTS:

i.   Under-giving is an insult to God.

ii.   Saying you don't have anything to give is untrue and offends God.

iii.   Not giving what he instructs you to give based on how he has blessed you renders your seed and yourself unacceptable to God.

iv.   God is all you need to have all your needs met.

v.   God does not need anything from you; you need everything from God.

vi.   Your giving does not add anything to God but it adds everything to you.

PROOF:

Psalms 50:5-15,

"Gather my saints together unto me; those that have made a covenant with me by sacrifice. And the heavens shall declare his righteousness: for God is judge himself. Selah. Hear, O my people, and I will speak; O Israel, and I will testify against thee: I am God, even thy God. I will not reprove thee for thy sacrifices or thy burnt offerings, to have been continually before me. I will take no bullock out of thy house, nor he goats out of thy folds. For every beast of the forest is mine, and the cattle upon a thousand hills. I know all the fowls of the mountains: and the wild beasts of

the field are mine. If I were hungry, I would not tell thee: for the world is mine, and the fulness thereof. Will I eat the flesh of bulls, or drink the blood of goats? Offer unto God thanksgiving; and pay thy vows unto the most High: And call upon me in the day of trouble: I will deliver thee, and thou shalt glorify me."

vii. GIVING WITH STINGINESS, WITHOUT JOY, UNWILLINGLY, GRUDGINGLY, WITH STOUT WORDS AND WITHOUT CHEERFULNESS IS UNACCEPTABLE TO GOD.
(Judges 8:25; Exodus 35:5,23; 2 Corinthians 8:3; 9:7; Malachi 3:13-14)

WHO, WHERE, WHAT, WHEN, HOW (THE WAY) TO GIVE???

WHO?
Luke 17:14,
"Go show yourself to the priest because there is an offering you must give to be perfected"

WHERE?
Deuteronomy 12:13-14,
"Take heed to thyself that thou offer not thy burnt offerings in every place that thou seest: But in the place which the Lord shall choose in one of thy tribes, there thou shalt offer thy burnt offerings, and there thou shalt do all that I command thee."

WHAT?

Deuteronomy 16:10,

"And thou shalt keep the feast of weeks unto the Lord thy God with a tribute of a freewill offering of thine hand, which thou shalt give unto the Lord thy God, according as the Lord thy God hath blessed thee:"

HOW and HOW OFTEN?

Deuteronomy 16:16-17,

"Three times in a year shall all thy males appear before the Lord thy God in the place which he shall choose; in the feast of unleavened bread, and in the feast of weeks, and in the feast of tabernacles: and they shall not appear before the Lord empty: EVERY MAN SHALL GIVE AS HE IS ABLE ACCORDING TO THE BLESSING OF THE LORD THY GOD WHICH HE HATH GIVEN THEE. Every man shall give as he is able, according to the blessing of the Lord thy God which he hath given thee."

WHICH KIND?

Deuteronomy 17:1,

"You shall not sacrifice to the Lord your God an ox or a sheep in which is a blemish, any defect whatever, for that is an abomination to the Lord your God."

YOU DETERMINE WHAT YOU RECEIVE BACK AND GIVE WITH PURPOSE, CHEERFULNESS AND WILLINGNESS!

2 Corinthians 9:6-9,

"But this I say, He which soweth sparingly shall reap also sparingly; and he which soweth bountifully shall reap also bountifully. Every man according as he purposeth in his heart, so let him give; not grudgingly, or of necessity: for God loveth a cheerful giver. And God is able to make all grace abound toward you; that ye, always having all sufficiency in all things, may abound to every good work: (As it is written, He hath dispersed abroad; he hath given to the poor: his righteousness remaineth for ever."

Listen:

FIRE ONLY COMES DOWN IN RESPONSE TO SACRIFICES!

22. Fire only comes down in response to sacrifices on specific altars!!

1 Kings 18:30-40,

"And Elijah said unto all the people, Come near unto me. And all the people came near unto him. And he repaired the altar of the Lord that was broken down. And Elijah took twelve stones, according to the number of the tribes of the sons of Jacob, unto whom the word of the Lord came, saying, Israel shall be thy name: And with the stones he built an altar in the name of the Lord: and he made a trench about the altar, as great as would contain two measures of seed. And he put the wood in order, and cut the bullock in pieces, and laid him on the wood, and said, Fill four barrels with water, and pour it on the burnt sacrifice, and on the wood. And he said,

Do it the second time. And they did it the second time. And he said, Do it the third time. And they did it the third time. And the water ran round about the altar; and he filled the trench also with water. And it came to pass at the time of the offering of the evening sacrifice, that Elijah the prophet came near, and said, Lord God of Abraham, Isaac, and of Israel, let it be known this day that thou art God in Israel, and that I am thy servant, and that I have done all these things at thy word. Hear me, O Lord, hear me, that this people may know that thou art the Lord God, and that thou hast turned their heart back again. Then the fire of the Lord fell, and consumed the burnt sacrifice, and the wood, and the stones, and the dust, and licked up the water that was in the trench. And when all the people saw it, they fell on their faces: and they said, The Lord, he is the God; the Lord, he is the God. And Elijah said unto them, Take the prophets of Baal; let not one of them escape. And they took them: and Elijah brought them down to the brook Kishon, and slew them there."

23. Altars are memorials

For Cornelius, the altars of prayer and alms were speaking all along and was rewarded in Acts 10:31,
"And said, Cornelius, thy prayer is heard, and thine alms are had in remembrance in the sight of God."

Resulting in an apostolic visitation from Peter.

24. Altars are places of remembrance with trans-generational impact.

Altars are memorials. The woman with the costly Alabaster ointment is still remembered till date as Jesus promised because of her sacrifice.

Mark 14:3-9,
"And being in Bethany in the house of Simon the leper, as he sat at meat, there came a woman having an alabaster box of ointment of spikenard very precious; and she brake the box, and poured it on his head. And there were some that had indignation within themselves, and said, Why was this waste of the ointment made? For it might have been sold for more than three hundred pence, and have been given to the poor. And they murmured against her. And Jesus said, Let her alone; why trouble ye her? She hath wrought a good work on me. For ye have the poor with you always, and whensoever ye will ye may do them good: but me ye have not always. She hath done what she could: she is come aforehand to anoint my body to the burying. Verily I say unto you, Wheresoever this gospel shall be preached throughout the whole world, this also that she hath done shall be spoken of for a memorial of her."

25. All Altars Eat Sacrifices And Speak After, In Your Favour.

Malachi 3:8-12,

"Will a man rob God? Yet ye have robbed me. But ye say, Wherein have we robbed thee? In tithes and offerings. Ye are cursed with a curse: for ye have robbed me, even this whole nation. Bring ye all the tithes into the storehouse, that there may be meat in mine house, and prove me now herewith, saith the Lord of hosts, if I will not open you the windows of heaven, and pour you out a blessing, that there shall not be room enough to receive it. And I will rebuke the devourer for your sakes, and he shall not destroy the fruits of your ground; neither shall your vine cast her fruit before the time in the field, saith the Lord of hosts. And all nations shall call you blessed: for ye shall be a delightsome land, saith the Lord of hosts."

a. The Lesser Powers Bow To The Greater Power From Seed On The Altar.

b. Dagon bowed to the greater power I.e. the Ark harbouring the presence of God in 1 Samuel 5:1-6, *"And the Philistines took the ark of God, and brought it from Ebenezer unto Ashdod. When the Philistines took the ark of God, they brought it into the house of Dagon, and set it by Dagon. And when they of Ashdod arose early on the morrow, behold, Dagon was fallen upon his face to the earth before the ark of the Lord. And they took Dagon, and set him in his place again. And when they arose early on the morrow morning, behold, Dagon was fallen upon his face to the ground before the ark of the Lord; and the head of Dagon and both the palms of his hands were cut off upon the threshold; only the stump of Dagon was left to him. Therefore neither the priests of Dagon, nor any that come into Dagon's house, tread on the threshold of Dagon in Ashdod unto this day. But the hand of the Lord was heavy upon them of Ashdod, and he destroyed them, and smote them with emerods, even Ashdod and the coasts thereof."*

c.   All power belongs to God and at the name of Jesus ever knee shall bow.

Psalms 62:11,
"God hath spoken once; twice have I heard this; that power belongeth unto God."

d.   The lesser bows to the greater always - Hebrews 7:7.

e.   God receives and keeps records of our tithes and our seeds on altars.

Hebrews 7:4-9,
"Now consider how great this man was, unto whom even the patriarch Abraham gave the tenth of the spoils. And verily they that are of the sons of Levi, who receive the office of the priesthood, have a commandment to take tithes of the people according to the law, that is, of their brethren, though they come out of the loins of Abraham: But he whose descent is not counted from them received tithes of Abraham,

and blessed him that had the promises. And without all contradiction the less is blessed of the better. And here men that die receive tithes; but there he receiveth them, of whom it is witnessed that he liveth. And as I may so say, Levi also, who receiveth tithes, payed tithes in Abraham."

Here, men that die receive the tithe but There (In Heaven) He receiveth and recordeth them...

God keeps records...

First of all tithe, give and then prove Him by Pleading your case... Not before. (Malachi 3:8-12)

Isaiah 41:21,
"Produce your cause, saith the Lord; bring forth your strong reasons, saith the King of Jacob."

Isaiah 43:26,
"Put me in remembrance: let us plead together: declare thou, that thou mayest be justified."

That's how the death sentence on Hezekiah in Isaiah 38, Dorcas in Acts 9, Lazarus in John 11 and The Roman Centurion's servant (Luke 7:2) were reversed. It was via their sacrifices and acts of service and alms.

A stage is where orators make speeches; an altar is where oracles are downloaded!

Chapter Four

35 DIFFERENCES BETWEEN A STAGE AND AN ALTAR

CAUTION:

To those of us who find ourselves on "stage" or platforms at church or see pulpits on stages, we will discover in this chapter:

i.   Why you shouldn't see your church and where the pulpit is situated as a platform, stage, podium, dais, rustrum or even just a pulpit but AN ALTAR.

ii. What you see a thing as or your understanding of what a thing or a product or person is, is what determines what you can get from it.

   a. He that receiveth a prophet in the name of a prophet shall receive a prophet's reward.

   b. Believe your prophets and you shall prosper. (2 Chronicles 20:20b)

    c. The Shunemite woman perceived Elisha as a prophet and did not get familiar with him. (2 Kings 4; Matthew 13:55; Mark 6:3)

    d. Jacob said: *"God was in this place and I knew it not..."* (Genesis 26:18)

iii. Don't take altars for granted or lightly; every church has an altar and that altar where the anointed or set man stands and speaks from, is his office and has a God who chose that altar as the place he meets them, speaks through them as his oracles, confirms their edicts, decrees and declarations, receive their prayers, tithes, offerings, sacrifices (Deuteronomy 12:13-14).

He speaks from that altar, to teach them, instruct them, guide them, lead them, direct them, and avenge them against all their adversaries as they call on him and give on that altar and confirms what He instructs them to say as confirmed in Isaiah 44:24-28.

God gave specific instructions 'Rear me an altar' to Abraham, Isaac, Jacob, David, Solomon, etc.

What's The Difference Between A Stage And An Altar?

1.   A stage is for performance; an altar is for worship.

a. A stage is for dancing to please men; an altar is for dancing to please God.

b. A stage is for dancing to please yourself, make you and others happy; an altar is for dancing to please God and provoke God's hand and judgment on your enemies (Psalm 149).

c. A stage is for singing praises that engage, excite, please and invite the audience to come to the floor to dance, and to the next party, gig or gathering; an altar is for singing praises that excite, please, invite and move God Himself to come down and inhabit and dwell in the praises of men and bless His people that the ends of the earth will fear Him.

Psalms 22:3,
"But thou art holy, O thou that inhabitest the praises of Israel."

Psalms 67:5-7,
"Let the people praise thee, O God; let all the people praise thee. Then shall the earth yield her increase; and God, even our own God, shall bless us. God shall bless us; and all the ends of the earth shall fear him."

No wonder David said, three times a day will I pray (Psalm 55:17) and seven times a day will I praise thee (Psalm 119:164). God gets angry with anyone that ridicules despises your praise of him to the extent he closes their womb because he hates it when people ridicule or despise people who do for Him what He cannot do for himself [Michal]. (2 Samuel 6:16,23)

2. A stage is for competition; an altar is for completion.

3. A stage is for personal applause; an altar is for God's glory.

4. A stage is for wooing the frantic crowd; an altar is for serenading the King of kings.

    [Serenade: a musical performance given to honour or express love for someone, often by one person.]

5. A stage is for dishing popular sentiment; an altar is for delivering heaven's edicts. (Genesis 22:16-18)

    [An EDICT is an Official order, decree or proclamation from someone in authority]

6. A stage is for selfish ambition; an altar is for selfless sacrifice. (2 Samuel 24:24; Genesis 22)

7. A stage is owned and manned by man; an altar is owned and supervised by a particular deity to whom it is erected and dedicated. (2 Samuel 24:18-25)

    Everyone has a god; make sure you know who yours is. In the battle between David and Goliath in 1 Samuel 17, the Bible says in verse 43, *"And the Philistine cursed David by his gods'* and David also said from verses 45-

47, '*but I come to you in the name of the Lord of hosts, the God of the armies of Israel, whom you have defied. This day the Lord will deliver you into my hand, and I will strike you down and cut off your head. And I will give the dead bodies of the host of the Philistines this day to the birds of the air and to the wild beasts of the earth, that all the earth may know that there is a God in Israel, and that all this assembly may know that the Lord saves not with sword and spear. For the battle is the Lord's, and he will give you into our hand.*"

The dimensions changed. It became a war of the altar of God and the altar of the Philistine gods. He came into this battle only armed with a slingshot and five stones; he had no sword to start with but he ended up cutting off the giant's head by his own sword. The ALTAR of the Lord of hosts prevailed.

MAKE SURE YOU HAVE A VERY SURE, VERY CERTAIN AND VERY ACTIVE ALTAR SPEAKING FOR YOU BEFORE YOU FACE OR ENTER CERTAIN BATTLES!!! It is triggered by your sacrifices on the altar including your church.

8. A stage is where everything must be perfect; an altar is where the imperfect are perfected.

9. A stage is where man ascends; an altar is where God descends. (Noah in Genesis 8:20-22; Solomon in 1 Kings 3; David in 2 Samuel 24; 1 Kings 17)

10. A stage pushes professionalism; an altar stresses spirituality.

11. A stage is all about how to project the right image; an altar is concerned about how to mould character. (Zechariah in Luke 1)

12. A stage is for fireworks display of human excellence, skill, and ingenuity; an altar is for the release of the divine purging fire of His holy presence. (Obadiah 17)

13. A stage is where stars gloat over the camera's glare; an altar is where sons lie prostrate, struck by heaven's glory. (Isaiah 6:1-8)

14. A stage is where a brilliant blaze of firecrackers illuminate the performer; an altar is where a bolt of heaven's fire disfigures the worshipper.

15. A stage is where living beings are showcased; an altar is where dead beings are offered. (Romans 12:1-2)

16. A stage is where artists pull out all the tricks of the trade to dazzle the crowd; an altar is where servants stay true to their call, so as to let the congregants draw closer to Jesus. (John 3:30)

17. A stage is where superstars hog the limelight; an altar is where everything pales into insignificance in light of the stunning bright Morning Star.

18. A stage is where man shouts his fame; an altar is where we shout His fame through His name. (Proverbs 18:10)

19. A stage is where man is lifted drawing men to himself; an altar is where He (Jesus) is lifted to draw men to himself. (John 12:32)

20. A stage is where self is exalted in fame; an altar is where self dies and the fame of Jesus is exalted. (Galatians 2:20)

21. A stage is where a man is consumed with fame; An altar is where the fire of God comes down to consume his sacrifice. (1 Kings 18)

22. A stage is where orators make speeches; an altar is where oracles are downloaded. (1 Peter 4:11)

23. A stage is for physical manifestations; an altar is for supernatural manifestations. (Exodus 8:19)

24. A stage is where we present our bodies and gifts to please and entertain men; An altar is where we present our bodies as living sacrifices. (Romans 12:1-2)

25. A stage is where performances and acts of men take place; an altar is where supernatural acts of God take place. (1 Samuel 5)

26. A stage is where flesh meets flesh; an altar is where spirits meet spirits. (Psalm 82:5)

27. A stage is where men meet men; an altar is where God meets men. (Genesis 22)

28. A stage is where humanity meets humanity; an altar is where divinity meets humanity and transforms him into an uncommon personality. (Exodus 3:8)

29. A stage is where men entertain men; an altar is where God transforms men. 'The Lord was here and I knew it not.' (Jacob in Genesis 28:16)

30. A stage is where man provokes applause, accolades and recognition; an altar is where you invoke and provoke the presence of God. (Acts 4:31; 1 Kings 18)

31. A stage is where physical revolutions are staged; an altar is where keys to supernatural revolutions and movements are provoked, initiated and sustained. (Acts 1:8; 2)

32. A stage is for promoting something spectacular; an altar is for provoking the supernatural. (2 Samuel 24:24)

33. A stage is for moving men; an altar is for moving God. (1 Kings 18)

34. A stage is for moving for men to move; an altar is for moving for God to move. (Genesis 12:1-3; 13:1-3; 22; 2 Samuel 24:24-25)

35. A stage is a place where your name remains the same in fame and popularity; an altar is where God changes your

name and when your enemies who had an intention to kill you, meet you, they rather embrace you because you have prevailed both with God and with men in battle. (Genesis 32&33; Jabez in 1 Chronicles 4:10)

'Never fight any man or woman of God who is sacrificial. It is God, you are fighting!

- Dr. Paul Enenche

Chapter Five

THE CHAPTER OF WARNINGS

Life Lessons:

This chapter contains things you must never do if you want to go higher.

Psalm 105:15,
'Saying TOUCH NOT MINE ANOINTED, AND DO MY PROPHETS NO HARM.'

Remember: WE MAY BE AGE MATES, BUT WE ARE NOT GRACE MATES!!

Hebrews 7:7,
"And without all contradiction the less is blessed of the better."

Proverbs 13:20,
'He that walketh with wise men shall be wise: but a companion of fools shall be destroyed.'

Proverbs 27:17,

(As) "Iron sharpeneth iron; so a man sharpeneth the countenance of his friend."

BEWARE, you are never found guilty of the following:

Offences, Unbelief and Over familiarity with Altars and Ministers and Priests That Serve Those Altars Can Cost You Dearly! AVOID IT AT ALL COST!

Matthew 13:54-58,

"And when he was come into his own country, he taught them in their synagogue, insomuch that they were astonished, and said, Whence hath this man this wisdom, and these mighty works? Is not this the carpenter's son? is not his mother called Mary? and his brethren, James, and Joses, and Simon, and Judas? And his sisters, are they not all with us? Whence then hath this man all these things? And they were offended in him. But Jesus said unto them, A prophet is not without honour, save in his own country, and in his own house. And he did not many mighty works there because of their unbelief."

Remember The LESSER IS BLESSED BY THE GREATER!

I. Abraham gave to Melchizedek.

Genesis 14:18-21,

"And Melchizedek king of Salem brought forth bread and

wine: and he was the priest of the most high God. And he blessed him, and said, Blessed be Abram of the most high God, possessor of heaven and earth: And blessed be the most high God, which hath delivered thine enemies into thy hand. And he gave him tithes of all. And the king of Sodom said unto Abram, Give me the persons, and take the goods to thyself.”

II. Joshua served Moses.

Deuteronomy 34:9,
“And Joshua the son of Nun was full of the spirit of wisdom; for Moses had laid his hands upon him: and the children of Israel hearkened unto him, and did as the Lord commanded Moses.”

III. Elisha served Elijah.

2 Kings 3:11,
“But Jehoshaphat said, Is there not here a prophet of the Lord, that we may enquire of the Lord by him? And one of the king of Israel’s servants answered and said, Here is Elisha the son of Shaphat, which poured water on the hands of Elijah.”

IV.   Ruth served Naomi.

When both of their husbands died, Naomi planned to return to Israel from Moab and encouraged Ruth to return to her mother’s family. Instead, Ruth answered,

"Don't urge me to leave you or to turn back from you. Where you go I will go, and where you stay I will stay. Your people will be my people and your God my God. Where you die I will die, and there I will be buried. May the Lord deal with me, be it ever so severely, if even death separates you and me" (Ruth 1:16-17)

Ruth apparently had made a commitment to follow Naomi's God as well. In her vow, she told Naomi, *"Your God, my God."* Naomi was convinced Ruth was serious, too. Ruth 1:18 notes,

"When Naomi realized that Ruth was determined to go with her, she stopped urging her."

40 THINGS YOU NEVER DO AGAINST ALTARS OR SACRIFICIAL PASTORS OR LEADERS WHO ARE ADDICTED TO SACRIFICES AND ALTARS, WHO SERVE AT YOUR ALTARS AND ARE SEEDS TO BOTH THEIR GENERATION AND GENERATIONS YET UNBORN (POSTERITY).

1. NEVER GIVE ANYHOW! ALWAYS GIVE WITH PURPOSE, AWE, HONOUR AND REVERENCE. GOD HAS A CHOICE AS TO WHOSE OFFERINGS HE ACCEPTS AND WHOSE HE REJECTS.

    Malachi 1:6,
    "A son honoureth his father, and a servant his master: if then I be a father, where is mine honour? and if I be a master, where is my fear? saith the Lord of hosts

unto you, O priests, that despise my name. And ye say, Wherein have we despised thy name?"

2. NEVER APPROACH ALTARS, TITHING, GIVING, SERVICE OF ANY KIND IN GOD'S HOUSE OR SACRIFICES loosely, haphazardly, lightly OR WITH DEFERENCE!!!

3. NEVER APPROACH SACRIFICES OR THE SACRIFICIAL ANYHOW!

4. NEVER APPROACH SACRIFICIAL AND ADDICTED GIVERS WHOM GOD CALLS MEN AND WOMEN AFTER HIS OWN HEART ANYHOW OR WITH DISRESPECT OR DISDAIN.

    Genesis 31:24,
    "And God came to Laban the Syrian in a dream by night, and said unto him, Take heed that thou speak not to Jacob either good or bad."

    God can speak to our enemies on our behalf and tell them how far they can go in dealing with us. (Isaiah 54:15-17)

    Laban said in Genesis 31:29,
    "It is in the power of my hand to do you hurt: but the God of your father spake unto me yesternight, saying, Take thou heed that thou speak not to Jacob either good or bad."

5. Never ever fight a man who understands and engages altars rightly, promptly and endlessly as an addiction. (Genesis 12, 14, 22)

6. Never speak evil of the sacrificial. Numbers 12:8, *"With him will I speak mouth to mouth, even apparently, and not in dark speeches; and the similitude of the Lord shall he behold: wherefore then were ye not afraid to speak against my servant Moses?"*

7. **Never ever fight a man or woman who always has sacrifices on his Father's (GOD) and his spiritual father's or mentors' altar speaking for him and never ever allow your spouse (husband or wife) to draw you away from your God-ordained leader, mentor, pastor or father. DON'T DO IT!!**

8. Never fight a man that is sacrificial, selfless, an addicted tither, giver or one sold out to God or for God in endless, selfless service. You may not just lose the battle or war against him, but, probably lose your life by dying in the process.

    They are not just human and don't just give offerings; they are a seed to their generation.

    i.   Dr. Paul Enenche said: 'Never fight any man or woman of God who is sacrificial. It is God, you are fighting!

Psalm 22:30-31,

"A seed shall serve him; it shall be accounted to the Lord for a generation. They shall come, and shall declare his righteousness unto a people that shall be born, that he hath done this."

ii. God has seeded them to their generation with special assignments and special messages which He's assigned them to do, preach and teach.

iii. He watches over them with godly jealousy and oversight.

iv. They Understand And Invoke The Power Of Altars!
1 Kings 18:36,

"And it came to pass at the time of the offering of the evening sacrifice, that Elijah the prophet came near, and said, Lord God of Abraham, Isaac, and of Israel, let it be known this day that thou art God in Israel, and that I am thy servant, and that I have done all these things at thy word. Hear me, O Lord, hear me, that this people may know that thou art the Lord God, and that thou hast turned their heart back again. Then the fire of the Lord fell, and consumed the burnt sacrifice, and the wood, and the stones, and the dust, and licked up the water that was in the trench. And when all the people saw it, they fell on their faces: and they said, The Lord, he is the God; the Lord, he is the God."

v. Heaven and angels recognise them and back them 120% and 24/7.

Isaiah 44:24-26,
"Thus saith the Lord, thy redeemer, and he that formed thee from the womb, I am the Lord that maketh all things; that stretcheth forth the heavens alone; that spreadeth abroad the earth by myself; That frustrateth the tokens of the liars, and maketh diviners mad; that turneth wise men backward, and maketh their knowledge foolish; That confirmeth the word of his servant, and performeth the counsel of his messengers that saith to Jerusalem, Thou shalt be inhabited; and to the cities of Judah, Ye shall be built, and I will raise up the decayed places thereof:"

vi. They are His emissaries and appointed carpenters to fray horns sent to scatter the church.

Zechariah 1:17-21,
"Cry yet, saying, Thus saith the Lord of hosts; My cities through prosperity shall yet be spread abroad; and the Lord shall yet comfort Zion, and shall yet choose Jerusalem. Then lifted I up mine eyes, and saw, and behold four horns. And I said unto the angel that talked with me, What be these? And he answered me, These are the horns which have scattered Judah, Israel, and Jerusalem. And the Lord shewed me four carpenters. Then said I, What come these to do? And he spake, saying, These are the horns which have

scattered Judah, so that no man did lift up his head: but these are come to fray them, to cast out the horns of the Gentiles, which lifted up their horn over the land of Judah to scatter it."

vii. They are the apple of His eye and He keeps them as the apple of His eye.

Deuteronomy 32:10,
"He found him in a desert land, and in the waste howling wilderness; he led him about, he instructed him, he kept him as the apple of his eye."

Psalms 17:8,
"Keep me as the apple of the eye, hide me under the shadow of thy wings."

Zechariah 2:8,
"For thus saith the Lord of hosts; After the glory hath he sent me unto the nations which spoiled you: for he that toucheth you toucheth the apple of his eye."

viii. God moves and instructs kings and authority figures to favour them.

Proverbs 21:1,
"The king's heart is in the hand of the Lord, as the rivers of water: he turneth it whithersoever he will."

You Need Understanding. Why?

Proverbs 21:16,

"The man that wandereth out of the way of understanding shall remain in the congregation of the dead."

ix. Everyone has a god and altars they bring their sacrifices to, who answer them in their hour of need as we saw in Jonah 1/2, David and Goliath in 1 Samuel 17:43-47 and Elijah instructing the heathen who were between two opinions to call on their gods in 1 Kings 18.

The question is 'What altars protect you, speak for you, defend you, eat your seed and respond to you, your tithes, prayers and your sacrificial seeds?'

Remember: You cannot withdraw from an altar what you have not given to.

Just as you cannot make withdrawals from any bank account you have not made deposits into, in the same vein, you cannot make withdrawals from an altar you have not sown into, upon, given to or sacrificed on. All altars have gods that answer to them.

x. All Altars have gods that receive their sacrifices. In 1 Kings 18:23-39, Elijah challenged the heathen to rear an altar and call on their gods and said: 'I will call on my God and the one who answers by fire, let him be God.' Their conclusion was: 'The Lord He is God', thus confirming God is an All Consuming fire leaving nothing behind and ALL POWER BELONGS TO GOD! (Hebrews 12:29; Psalm 62:11)

9. Never dishonour the anointed or the anointing on a servant of God because the anointing destroys yokes and removes burdens including things and people who become yokes and burdens. So, when you become a yoke and burden in the life of a servant of God, the anointing on him can destroy you and remove you. Be very careful! Their silence does not mean you are getting away with it. What it means is: God will avenge them!!

    Isaiah 10:27,
    "And it shall come to pass in that day, that his burden shall be taken away from off thy shoulder, and his yoke from off thy neck, and the yoke shall be destroyed because of the anointing."

Warning: Don't go there!!

10. Never forget the Levites who Sacrifice so much on your behalf.

     Deuteronomy 14:27,
     "And the Levite that is within thy gates; thou shalt not forsake him; for he hath no part nor inheritance with thee."

INGRATITUDE IS WORSE THAN WITCHCRAFT!

11. Never break the pot that once gave you water.

12. Never bite the hands that once fed you.

13. Never despise the home that once gave you shelter.

14. Never punch holes in the umbrella that once gave you cover.

15. Never insult the breasts that once gave you pleasure.

16. Never correct, never be rude and never point an accusing finger at a father figure who once birthed, raised, covered, counselled, protected and taught you what he knew.

17. Never join forces, entertain or associate in any shape or form with any one like Absalom, Demas or Ahithophel who is diagonally or diametrically opposed to, against, rude to or who curses, resists, hates, plots the downfall, destruction or who is critical of your church or a spiritual authority figure, much more your leader. That is your Ark and that's your Covering. Never jump off that ship prematurely. (Genesis 5:32-10:1)

     Proverbs 20:19-21,
     "He that goeth about as a talebearer revealeth secrets: therefore meddle not with him that flattereth with his lips. Whoso curseth his father or his mother, his lamp

shall be put out in obscure darkness. An inheritance may be gotten hastily at the beginning; but the end thereof shall not be blessed."

Stay Clear Of Them!!! Their Altars may cry out and speak against you and avenge them.

18. NEVER DO ANYTHING EVIL TO THEM THAT WILL PROMPT THEM TO SAY: "I HAVE REMOVED MY COVERING FROM YOU OR WASHED MY HANDS OFF YOU" YOU ARE ON YOUR OWN. NEVER DO ANYTHING EVIL TO ALLOW THOSE WORDS TO COME OUT OF THEIR MOUTH. NEVER LET THEM SHAKE THE DUST OFF THEIR FEET AGAINST YOU (Matthew 10:14).

19. Never ever malign the church that once gave you fire and your spiritual feed. If for now, you have outgrown their usefulness, leave them intact and go quietly and honourably. For it may be the time and season of breakthrough there for others also. Be careful how you close a door.

   Never ever bang it; you may need to walk through that same door tomorrow or may need to be rescued by that father figure or pastor you left, despised, hurt, betrayed, defamed, accused, maligned and tried to destroy on your way out because you thought it was your season and thought you had arrived. Ask Lot!!

That church may no longer be your church but, is still someone's home and that pastor may no longer be your pastor but is still someone's father, someone's pastor and still someone's treasure irrespective of what you think. The way you join a church no one remembers, but the way you leave, everyone will remember. Be Very Careful!!! What you sow is what you will reap and remember He that sows the wind shall surely reap the whirlwind. (Galatians 6:7; Hosea 8:7)

20. Never curse your father or mother or a father figure or mother figure who once did you good and officiated your birth, dedications and your marriage i.e. wedding; spiritual and physical and that of your children; you are digging your early grave. Remember: Those same spiritual authority figures are licensed to officiate at births, officiate at weddings and officiate at burials too. Don't make that burial ceremony yours!

Proverbs 20:20-21,
"Whoso curseth his father or his mother, his lamp shall be put out in obscure darkness. An inheritance may be gotten hastily at the beginning; but the end thereof shall not be blessed."

The scriptures cannot be broken. (John 10:35) You cannot do anything against the truth but for the truth. (2 Corinthians 13:8) Dishonour brings a curse. (Malachi 1:6-14; 6:4)

21. Never dishonour a teacher, pastor or father who taught you what and all you know now to bring you where you are now.

22. Never criticise what you don't understand. Just because you don't understand, does not make it wrong bad or evil. Never try to understand what you don't or cannot understand and never try to explain what you cannot explain. It's beyond your pay grade. Avoid the 'weightier' matters and 'MIND YOUR OWN BUSINESS' (Matthew 23:23).

23. Never entertain, tolerate or associate with those who belong to the 'Proverbs 6:16-19 club' or those who cause division. Evil communication corrupts good manners.

    Romans 16:17-18,
    "Now I beseech you, brethren, mark them which cause divisions and offences contrary to the doctrine which ye have learned; and avoid them. For they that are such serve not our Lord Jesus Christ, but their own belly; and by good words and fair speeches deceive the hearts of the simple."

    Proverbs 6:16-19,
    "These six things doth the Lord hate: yea, seven are an abomination unto him: A proud look, a lying tongue and hands that shed innocent blood, An heart that deviseth wicked imaginations, feet that be swift in running to

mischief. *A false witness that speaketh lies, and he that soweth discord among brethren."*

1 Corinthians 15:33-34,
"Be not deceived: evil communications corrupt good manners. Awake to righteousness, and sin not; for some have not the knowledge of God: I speak this to your shame."

Don't believe your CV OR RESUME. YOU CAN BE CORRUPTED!

1 Corinthians 10:12,
"Wherefore let him that thinketh he standeth take heed lest he fall."

24. Never do a 'Dathan and Abiram' on an elder or spiritual authority figure who sends for you whether you think you are right or have been wronged. Never ever be rude, insolent or disrespect, disdain, despise or dishonour them or their office.

    Numbers 16:12,
    "Then Moses summoned Dathan and Abiram, the sons of Eliab. But they said, "We will not come!"

25. Never fight a man or woman or leader who is sacrificial and selfless. Because, it is God you are fighting. Never fight a leader who is more sacrificial, selfless, useful and necessary to God than you. You will never win. Never

fight a sacrificially giving pastor; your life will be taken to preserve his.

26. Never become proud and ignorantly or purposefully invite leprosies into your body by criticising your Moses as Miriam and Aaron did.

Numbers 12:2-3,
"And they said, Hath the Lord indeed spoken only by Moses? hath he not spoken also by us? And the Lord heard it. (Now the man Moses was very meek, above all the men which were upon the face of the earth)"

Numbers 12:8-10,
"With him will I speak mouth to mouth, even apparently, and not in dark speeches; and the similitude of the Lord shall he behold: wherefore then were ye not afraid to speak against my servant Moses? And the anger of the Lord was kindled against them; and he departed. And the cloud departed from off the tabernacle; and, behold, Miriam became leprous, white as snow: and Aaron looked upon Miriam, and, behold, she was leprous."

27. No matter how high you rise, never be ungrateful and never ever equate yourself with the one who raised you. **Remember: WE MAY BE AGE MATES, BUT WE ARE NOT GRACE MATES!!**

Don't make that mistake. We may be age mates, but we are not grace mates. It is grace that makes the difference.

The grace on a gift or gifted person or leader is what makes all the difference between one leader and another. Never ever make that mistake!

28. **When it comes to Spiritual things, in relation to the fivefold ministry, church, management, leadership and ministry-related matters in general, never look at or relate to or with a servant of God according to his humanity but rather, according to HIS DIVINITY – HIS GOD-SIDE NOT HIS MAN-SIDE or else you will miss out on a whole lot i.e. the graces, anointing, wisdom, insight and virtues they carry for you.**

29. **If you want or desire to grow old gracefully, never speak against an old man or the aged.** If you don't honour the aged, you will never become the aged or be honoured in your old age. Never criticise or oppose or undermine the wise actions, decisions and choices of those who have gone ahead of you which you don't understand. Remember: Young people think old people are fools but old people know that young people are fools.

30. If you want to become an elder in life, never disrespect, dishonour, speak against or harm anyone older than you or an elderly person or an elder or leader in ministry; it's a taboo! It is never done; Do a Bible search and ask

Dathan, Abiram, Achan, Korah, Absalom, Ahithophel, Alexander the coppersmith, Demas, Judas and Lucifer.

31. If you want or desire to be rich and prosperous in life and ministry, never speak evil of or against a rich and prosperous person, mentor, minister or father figure in ministry. What you don't respect you cannot attract. You Cannot And Will Not Attract What You Despise Or Speak Against! If you want to become an exceptional parent, never judge, resist, criticise or speak against any parent. You Cannot Become Or Get What You Criticise!!

32. If you want to be successful in life, never criticise, demean, undermine or speak against the successful. Don't try to understand what you don't understand or explain what you cannot explain; rather, ask the right questions and get the right answers from the right people. Just because you don't understand the source of something or someone's success, does not make it wrong. Instead of aiming for or criticising the glory, settle down and understand the story behind the glory.

Remember: THERE IS NO STAR WITHOUT A SCAR! Underneath Every Star, Is A Scar!! It is Scars, That Make Stars!!

33. If you want to attract respect, i.e. be respected, then, never disrespect what you want to attract. What you don't respect, you won't attract.

1 Thessalonians 5:12-13,

'And we beseech you, brethren, to know them which labour among you, and are over you in the Lord, and admonish you; And to esteem them very highly in love for their work's sake. And be at peace among yourselves.'

34. If you want or desire to be blessed, never speak against the blessed. If you want to become a leader one day, never criticise or speak against a leader ahead of you. You don't become what you criticise. You end up doing worse than the people you criticise and accuse. Rather, highly esteem those ahead of you.

35. If you want things to be well with you and to live a long productive and fulfilled life, honour your biological parents and obey your spiritual parents i.e. Your pastors. Period!

    The only thing spiritual parents i.e. Pastors, Prophets, Apostles, Teachers, Evangelists owe you Are Instructions!!

    Ephesians 6:1-3,

    "Children, obey your parents in the Lord: for this is right. Honour thy father and mother; (which is the first commandment with promise;) That it may be well with thee, and thou mayest live long on the earth."

36. Never withhold any good thing from a father figure, priest, mentor or the altar who helped raise you, made you and is still making you, when it is within your power to do so. WHEN YOU BECOME BIG, TRACE YOUR FOUNDATION.

37. Never violate any of the following from 1 Corinthians 9:8-14,
    "Never muzzle the mouth of the ox that treadeth out the corn. Doth God take care for oxen? Or saith he it altogether for our sakes? For our sakes, no doubt, this is written: that he that ploweth should plow in hope; and that he that thresheth in hope should be partaker of his hope."

38. Never make a big deal or complain about reciprocating the input of spiritual gifts in your life. If we have sown unto you spiritual things, is it a great thing if we shall reap your carnal things? If others be partakers of this power over you, are not we rather?

39. Never forget that they which minister about holy things, live of the things of the temple? and they which wait at the altar are partakers with the altar? Even so hath the Lord ordained that they which preach the gospel should live of the gospel.

40. Never violate Romans 15:27,

   'It hath pleased them verily; and their debtors they are. For if the Gentiles have been made partakers of their spiritual things, their duty is also to minister unto them in carnal things.'

An altar is a place where divinity comes upon humanity to make them an uncommon personality!

Chapter Six

THE POWER AND SIGNIFICANCE OF ALTARS

The Power and Significance of Altars

Death was swallowed up in victory at the altar of sacrifice.

1 Corinthians 15:54,
"So when this corruptible shall have put on incorruption, and this mortal shall have put on immortality, then shall be brought to pass the saying that is written, Death is swallowed up in victory."

101 MIRACULOUS BENEFITS OF ALTARS:

1. An altar is a place where humanity meets divinity. (Exodus 25:22)

2. An altar is a place where the natural meets the supernatural and bows. (1 Samuel 5)

3. An altar is a place where men's voice provoke, hear and submit to God's voice. (Isaiah 30:21)

4. An altar is a place of divine encounters. (Acts 9)

5. An altar is erected for the offering of sacrifices to activate that altar. When you take a sacrifice to the altar, you invoke and provoke the presence of the spirits or God. (1 Kings 3:3-15; Isaiah 11:1-3)

6. Altars are places of divine exchange and where barrenness is permanently terminated. (Luke 1)

7. Altars are places where destinies are decided. (Exodus 3:1-17)

8. Altars are places where sworn blessings are released. (Genesis 22)

9. Altars are places where generational leaders are appointed and released. (Genesis 12; 22)

10. Altars are places in history where revolutionaries and deliverers are born and released. (Exodus 3:1-17)

11. Altars are places of remembrance. (Cornelius [Acts 10:1]; woman with alabaster ointment [Matthew 26:7]; Psalm 20:1-4)

12. Altars are places of ascending and descending. (Genesis 28:11-22)

13. Altars are where heaven answers earth.

14. Altars are where heaven responds to earth.

15. Altars are where heavenly rewards respond to earthly sacrifices.

16. Altars are where incense through prayers and sacrificial offerings ascend as a sweet smell in God's nostrils to provoke his supplies. (Philippians 4:19)

17. Altars are where the heavens are provoked to open and remain continually open. (Malachi 3)

18. Altars are where heavenly responses are triggered. (1 Kings 3:3-5)

19. Altars are where what leaves earth determines what leaves heaven. (1 Kings 18)

20. Altars are where God is smoked out of heaven to ask us what we want him to do for us. (2 Chronicles 25:9)

21. Altars are where impossibilities become possible.

22. Altars are the platform for triggering and provoking the supernatural, the miraculous and signs and wonders. (1 Kings 18:31-39; 2 Kings 1:10,12)

23. Altars trigger the inexplainable, undeniable, indescribable, unforgettable, indisputable, unbelievable, unimaginable, inexplainable, incomprehensible, uncontainable, inexhaustible invaluable, unmatchable, undetectable, unstoppable and incomparable. (Deuteronomy 29:29)

24. Altars are where the irreparables are repaired and the irreplaceables are replaced. (Acts 3)

25. Altars are where dysfunctional, old or dead human organs are totally replaced with new ones. (Acts 10:38)

26. Altars are where the untreatable are treated.

27. Altars are where the unhealables are totally healed. (Mark 5)

28. Altars are where the irrecoverable are recovered.

29. Altars are where new organs are totally recreated. (Mark 10:46-52)

30. Altars are where special and creative miracles occur. (Matthew 12:13)

31. Altars are where God descends to give an open cheque to those who give you sacrificial offerings and ask whatever man wants him to do for them. (1 Kings 3:3)

32. Altars are where irrevocable sworn blessings are pronounced, decreed and declared irreversible. (Genesis 22)

33. Altars are where all controversies are settled.

34. Altars are where acceptable sacrifices of a sweet smell and aroma ascend and divine help and allocations descend. (Genesis 8:20-22; Philippians 4:18-19)

35. Altars are places where dreams are sealed. (1 Kings 3:3-15)

36. Altars are places where sacrificial seeds with generational significance and impact are sown. (Genesis 22)

37. Altars are where even curses pronounced by God are overturned permanently in both our favour and for generations yet unborn. (Genesis 8:20-22; John 3:16)

38. Altars are where fire responds to earth to consume sacrifices. Elijah (1 Kings 18:36-38)

39. Altars are where declarations, demands, decrees and invocations of prophetic voices are given heavenly accreditation, weight, credibility and confirmation. (1 Kings 18:36-39)

40. Altars are where the God that answereth by fire descends with pomp, might and power to demonstrate and confirm he is God indeed. (1 Kings 18:24,38)

41. Altars are places where fire licks up water contrary to and in defiance of conventional science.

    1 Kings 18:38,
    "Then the fire of the lord fell, and consumed the burnt sacrifice, and the wood, and the stones, and the dust, and licked up the water that was in the trench."

42. Altars are places where divine protocol defies, takes over and makes nonsense of natural protocol. (Mark 1:35-43)

43. Altars are places where God's power is clearly demonstrated to the astonishment of all our enemies and the heathen. (1 Kings 18:22-38)

44. Altars are where God leaves man in no doubt that there is no God like our God. (1 Kings 8:23)

45. Altars are where God proves that all power belongs to him and him alone. (Psalm 62:11)

46. Altars are places where God leaves men and all forces of darkness in no doubt that he is sovereign and the God of the entire universe. (Psalm 24:1)

47. Altars are where God demonstrates that he has the final say, the final word and the final verdict to rule in our favour. (Isaiah 55)

48. Altars are where favour is entreated. (Psalm 45:12; Psalm 102:13-15)

49. Altars make the difference between a life of poverty or riches, sickness or health, curses or blessings, peace or war, long life or premature death, acceptable offerings or unacceptable offerings. Examples of the life and giving records and attitudes of Jacob, Esau, Cain & Abel.

50. Altars are places of major determinations. (Luke 1; 1 Samuel 1)

51. Altars provoke alterations. (Exodus 34:29-35)

52. Altars are where the inalterables are permanently altered. (Matthew 17:1-13)

53. Altars are where the unsolvables are solved. (Matthew 15:37)

54. Altars are where dead things and dead bodies come back to life. (John 11)

55. Altars are where permanent answers replace questions and question marks. (Mark 9:23)

56. Altars are where generational injunctions of impotency are terminated in a second. (John 5)

57. Altars are where terminal diseases are terminally terminated. (Matthew 14:36)

58. Altars are where barrenness is permanently destroyed. (Exodus 23:25-26)

59. Altars are where demonic invocations are overthrown, overruled, overturned and rendered permanently powerless, useless and totally annihilated. (Luke 10:19; John 19:30)

60. Altars are where generational curses and national plagues of the greatest magnitude are permanently averted, deleted, destroyed, stayed and terminated. (2 Samuel 24)

61. Selfless sacrifices on altars are accounted for generations. *"A seed shall serve him; it shall be accounted to the Lord for a generation."* (Psalms 22:30)

62. Seeds sacrificed and vows made on altars sometimes provoke answers that prayer does not trigger. (Hannah in 1 Samuel; 2 Samuel 24; 1 Kings 3)

63. An altar is a place of sacrifices. (1 Kings 18)

64. An altar is a place of giving offerings. (Genesis 8:20-22)

65. An altar is a place of divine irreversible exchange. (Genesis 22; 2 Samuel 24; Luke 1)

66. An altar is a place where spirits come with spiritual things and humans exchange it with physical things i.e. the tangible is exchanged for the intangible.

67. An altar is a place of donations.

68. An altar is a place where donations are exchanged for heavenly decrees and irreversible blessings. (Genesis 22)

69. An altar is a place where divinity comes upon humanity to make them an uncommon personality. (1 Samuel 10:6)

70. An altar is a place of invocations.

71. An altar is a place of defence and justification where you plead your case. (Isaiah 41:21; 43:26)

72. An altar is a place of divine appearances.

73. An altar is a place of angelic appearances. (Genesis 18)

74. An altar is a place of permanent alterations.

75. An altar is a place of divine interventions, where our enemies are given miscarried wombs and dry breasts as punishment for their wicked acts.

Hosea 9:14,

"Give them, O lord: what wilt thou give? Give them a miscarrying womb and dry breasts."

76. An altar is a place of supernatural interventions, where the wickedness of the wicked comes to an end via prayer altars and God establishes the just. (Psalm 7:9)

77. An altar is a place of the release of supernatural intelligence. (Luke 21:15; 1 Kings 3:3-15)

78. An altar is a place of divine settlement. (Genesis 22:9-12)

79. An altar is a place of divine downloads.

80. An altar is a place of divine acceleration and speedy answers to prayer. (Isaiah 65:24)

81. An altar is a place of generational sworn and irreversible blessings. (Genesis 12:1-3; 22)

82. An altar is a place of divine injunctions, where spells, enchantments and divinations boomerang back into the camp of our enemies. (Numbers 23:23)

83. An altar is a place of undeniable proofs.

84. An altar is a place of divine consequences. (Acts 5:1 - Ananias and Sapphira)

85. An altar is a place of God's acknowledgement. (Genesis 22:12)

86. An altar is a place of God's appearance. (Bethel - Genesis 28)

87. An altar is a place where God speaks for you because altars have voices and speak for you. Altars speak for us or against us our haters, enemies and adversaries.

   Exodus 2:24,
   "God heard their groaning and he remembered his covenant with Abraham, with Isaac and with Jacob."

88. An altar is a gate; wherever you see altars, there is a gate where spirits access. (Genesis 24:60)

89. An altar is a place where vows are made. (Job 22:25-28)

90. An altar is a place where God responds to vows made earnestly with speed swiftly. (1 Samuel 1:10-19)

91. An altar is a place where covenants are made. (Psalm 89:34)

92. An altar is a place where oaths are sworn. (Genesis 22:16; Psalm 89:3,35; 119:106; Isaiah 14:24; 45:23; 54:9; Jeremiah 11:5; Hebrews 4:3)

93. An altar is a place where sworn blessings are pronounced in response to sacrificial offerings. Example: Isaac, your only son, the one you love. (Genesis 22)

   An altar is a place where God swears exclusively by himself to bless selfless, sacrificial seed-sowers with sworn blessings. (Genesis 22)

94. An altar is a place where something positive from heaven answers to something positive from the earth. (2 Samuel 24:24)

95. Altars a places that receive and honour sacrificial services and even reverse sicknesses unto death. (Luke 7:1-5)

96. Altars terminate generational poverty and disgrace. (Gideon and altars in Judges 6).

97. Altars are places where offerings are pronounced or judged acceptable or unacceptable. (Cain and Abel in Genesis 4)

98. Altars release incense towards heaven. When the angel takes the censer, and fills it with fire of the altar, and cast it into the earth: there arise voices, and thunderings, and lightnings, and an earthquake. (Revelation 8:3-5 KJV)

99. Altars emit sweet smells and aromas towards heaven and provoke God's undivided attention and speedy life-transforming responses. (Revelation 8:3-5)

100. Sacrifices on altars smoke God out of heaven. (1 Kings 3:3; 18)

101. Altars that receive, record, eat, consume, swallow our sacrifices, reverse death sentences including even God-pronounced sentences. Hezekiah's death sentence revoked through sacrificial service. (Isaiah 38)

*A Sacrifice Is Not A
Sacrifice, Until It Costs You
Something!*

Chapter Seven

THE POWER OF SACRIFICES

How To Invoke The Power Of Altars Through The Power Of Sacrifices

First statement: Sacrifice Is Not Sacrifice Until It Costs You Something!

Isaiah 49:24-26,

"Shall the prey be taken from the mighty, or the lawful captive delivered? But thus saith the Lord, Even the captives of the mighty shall be taken away, and the prey of the terrible shall be delivered: for I will contend with him that contendeth with thee, and I will save thy children. And I will feed them that oppress thee with their own flesh; and they shall be drunken with their own blood, as with sweet wine: and all flesh shall know that I the Lord am thy Saviour and thy Redeemer, the mighty One of Jacob."

This is God's promise to all those who understand and sacrifice on God's designated altars.

Psalm 142:7,

"Bring my soul out of prison, that I may praise thy name: the righteous shall compass me about; for thou shalt deal bountifully with me."

From 1 Corinthians 10:1,14,19-20, Paul was saying, I would not have you ignorant about the difference between sacrificing to idols and sacrificing to God; there is a vast difference. Ignorance is a killer and is the most affordable commodity in the Market.

WHAT IS THE DEFINITION OF SACRIFICE?

What Is A Sacrifice?

The definition of the word SACRIFICE from Advance Learners Dictionary:

I.   The giving up of something of great value to oneself for a special purpose or to benefit someone else.

II. So, a sacrifice is giving up something beneficial, profitable or of immense value to you, not for your benefit but for the benefit of a special purpose or someone else.

FACTS AND BIBLICAL EXAMPLES ABOUT SACRIFICES:

1.   So: A SACRIFICE IS NOT A SACRIFICE UNTIL IT COSTS YOU SOMETHING.

Psalms 126:5-6,

"They that sow in tears shall reap in joy. He that goeth forth and weepeth, bearing precious seed, shall doubtless come again with rejoicing, bringing his sheaves with him."

2 Samuel 24:24-25,

"And the king said unto Araunah, Nay; but I will surely buy it of thee at a price: neither will I offer burnt offerings unto the Lord my God of that which doth cost me nothing. So David bought the threshingfloor and the oxen for fifty shekels of silver. And David built there an altar unto the Lord, and offered burnt offerings and peace offerings. So the Lord was intreated for the land, and the plague was stayed from Israel."

Luke 14:25-27,

"And there went great multitudes with him: and he turned, and said unto them, If any man come to me, and hate not his father, and mother, and wife, and children, and brethren, and sisters, yea, and his own life also, he cannot be my disciple. And whosoever doth not bear his cross, and come after me, cannot be my disciple."

2.   It Cost God His Only Begotten Son To Save Us.

John 3:16,

"For God so loved the world, that he gave his only begotten Son, that whosoever believeth in him should not perish, but have everlasting life."

3.   It Cost Jesus Everything To Save Us.

John 10:14-18,
"I am the good shepherd, and know my sheep, and am known of mine. As the Father knoweth me, even so know I the Father: and I lay down my life for the sheep. And other sheep I have, which are not of this fold: them also I must bring, and they shall hear my voice; and there shall be one fold, and one shepherd. Therefore doth my Father love me, because I lay down my life, that I might take it again. No man taketh it from me, but I lay it down of myself. I have power to lay it down, and I have power to take it again. This commandment have I received of my Father."

John 12:32,
"And I, if I be lifted up from the earth, will draw all men unto me."

John 15:13,
"Greater love hath no man than this, that a man lay down his life for his friends."

4.   Being Given A Name Above Every Other Name Was Very Costly.

Philippians 2:5-11,
"Let this mind be in you, which was also in Christ Jesus: Who, being in the form of God, thought it not robbery to be equal with God: But made himself of no reputation, and took upon him the form of a servant, and was

made in the likeness of men: And being found in fashion as a man, he humbled himself, and became obedient unto death, even the death of the cross. Wherefore God also hath highly exalted him, and given him a name which is above every name: That at the name of Jesus every knee should bow, of things in heaven, and things in earth, and things under the earth; And that every tongue should confess that Jesus Christ is Lord, to the glory of God the Father."

5. Just As Jesus Endured Hardness, As Part Of The Sacrifice, So Must We.

Hebrews 12:1-2,
"Wherefore seeing we also are compassed about with so great a cloud of witnesses, let us lay aside every weight, and the sin which doth so easily beset us, and let us run with patience the race that is set before us, Looking unto Jesus the author and finisher of our faith; who for the joy that was set before him endured the cross, despising the shame, and is set down at the right hand of the throne of God."

2 Timothy 2:3-4,
"Thou therefore endure hardness, as a good soldier of Jesus Christ. No man that warreth entangleth himself with the affairs of this life; that he may please him who hath chosen him to be a soldier."

2 Timothy 4:5-6,

"But watch thou in all things, endure afflictions, do the work of an evangelist, make full proof of thy ministry. For I am now ready to be offered, and the time of my departure is at hand."

6. It Cost Abraham The Willing and Prompt Sacrifice Of His First And Only Son Whom He Loved Dearly And Waited 25 years For, To Provoke Sworn Blessings.

Genesis 22:2-3,

"And he said, Take now thy son, thine only son Isaac, whom thou lovest, and get thee into the land of Moriah; and offer him there for a burnt offering upon one of the mountains which I will tell thee of. And Abraham rose up early in the morning, and saddled his ass, and took two of his young men with him, and Isaac his son, and clave the wood for the burnt offering, and rose up, and went unto the place of which God had told him."

Genesis 22:12,

"And he said, Lay not thine hand upon the lad, neither do thou any thing unto him: for now I know that thou fearest God, seeing thou hast not withheld thy son, thine only son from me."

7. Sworn Blessings Are Not Free; They Are Provoked By Sacrifices.

Genesis 22:15-18,

"And the angel of the Lord called unto Abraham out of heaven the second time, And said, By myself have I sworn, saith the Lord, for because thou hast done this thing, and hast not withheld thy son, thine only son: That in blessing I will bless thee, and in multiplying I will multiply thy seed as the stars of the heaven, and as the sand which is upon the sea shore; and thy seed shall possess the gate of his enemies; And in thy seed shall all the nations of the earth be blessed; because thou hast obeyed my voice."

8. We Were Purchased By His Precious Sacrificial Blood.

Galatians 2:20,

"I am crucified with Christ: nevertheless I live; yet not I, but Christ liveth in me: and the life which I now live in the flesh I live by the faith of the Son of God, who loved me, and gave himself for me."

1 Corinthians 6:20,

"For ye are bought with a price: therefore glorify God in your body, and in your spirit, which are God's."

1 Corinthians 7:23,

"Ye are bought with a price; be not ye the servants of men."

1 Peter 1:18-19,

"Forasmuch as ye know that ye were not redeemed with corruptible things, as silver and gold, from your

vain conversation received by tradition from your fathers; But with the precious blood of Christ, as of a lamb without blemish and without spot:"

9. Death To Self Is The Fertiliser or Manure For Greatness in Life.

    John 12:23-26,
    "And Jesus answered them, saying, The hour is come, that the Son of man should be glorified. Verily, verily, I say unto you, Except a corn of wheat fall into the ground and die, it abideth alone: but if it die, it bringeth forth much fruit. He that loveth his life shall lose it; and he that hateth his life in this world shall keep it unto life eternal. If any man serve me, let him follow me; and where I am, there shall also my servant be: if any man serve me, him will my Father honour."

10. We Must Become Living Sacrifices Which Makes It Easy To Part With Our Resources.

    Romans 12:1-2,
    "I beseech you therefore, brethren, by the mercies of God, that ye present your bodies a living sacrifice, holy, acceptable unto God, which is your reasonable service. And be not conformed to this world: but be ye transformed by the renewing of your mind, that ye may prove what is that good, and acceptable, and perfect, will of God."

Philippians 1:21,
"For to me to live is Christ, and to die is gain."

11. Until We Give Ourselves Wholly, Our Profiting Will Not Appear To All.

    1 Timothy 4:15,
    "Meditate upon these things; give thyself wholly to them; that thy profiting may appear to all."

    1 Corinthians 15:10,
    "But by the grace of God I am what I am: and his grace which was bestowed upon me was not in vain; but I laboured more abundantly than they all: yet not I, but the grace of God which was with me."

12. There are only two altars i.e. altar unto God or altar up to gods (idols) because satan is a copy cat. (Judges 6)

13. God and Jesus recognise sacrificial offerings.

    Mark 12:41-44,
    "And Jesus sat over against the treasury, and beheld how the people cast money into the treasury: and many that were rich cast in much. And there came a certain poor widow, and she threw in two mites, which make a farthing. And he called unto him his disciples, and saith unto them, Verily I say unto you, That this poor widow hath cast more in, than all they which have cast into the treasury: For all they did cast in of their abundance;

but she of her want did cast in all that she had, even all her living."

14. Altars speak for you. God recognises sacrifices.

Genesis 4:3-5,
"And in process of time it came to pass, that Cain brought of the fruit of the ground an offering unto the Lord. And Abel, he also brought of the firstlings of his flock and of the fat thereof. And the Lord had respect unto Abel and to his offering: But unto Cain and to his offering he had not respect."

Hebrews 11:4,
"By faith Abel offered unto God a more excellent sacrifice than Cain, by which he obtained witness that he was righteous, God testifying of his gifts: and by it he being dead yet speaketh."

And Cain was very wroth, and his countenance fell. [Abel and Cain; woman with alabaster ointment; Cornelius as we saw in the previous chapters.]

15. Altars, vows and sacrifices protect you from evil, spells, enchantments, injunctions, etc.

1 Samuel 1:10-12,
"And she was in bitterness of soul, and prayed unto the Lord, and wept sore. And she vowed a vow, and said, O Lord of hosts, if thou wilt indeed look on the affliction of thine handmaid, and remember me, and not forget

thine handmaid, but wilt give unto thine handmaid a man child, then I will give him unto the Lord all the days of his life, and there shall no razor come upon his head. And it came to pass, as she continued praying before the Lord, that Eli marked her mouth."

1 Samuel 1:17-21,
"Then Eli answered and said, Go in peace: and the God of Israel grant thee thy petition that thou hast asked of him. And she said, Let thine handmaid find grace in thy sight. So the woman went her way, and did eat, and her countenance was no more sad. And they rose up in the morning early, and worshipped before the Lord, and returned, and came to their house to Ramah: and Elkanah knew Hannah his wife; and the Lord remembered her. Wherefore it came to pass, when the time was come about after Hannah had conceived, that she bare a son, and called his name Samuel, saying, Because I have asked him of the Lord. And the man Elkanah, and all his house, went up to offer unto the Lord the yearly sacrifice, and his vow."

16. Decrees are made with sacrifices at altars which become memorials for you.

Matthew 26:6-13,
"Now when Jesus was in Bethany, in the house of Simon the leper, There came unto him a woman having an alabaster box of very precious ointment, and poured it on his head, as he sat at meat. But when his disciples

saw it, they had indignation, saying, To what purpose is this waste? For this ointment might have been sold for much, and given to the poor. When Jesus understood it, he said unto them, Why trouble ye the woman? for she hath wrought a good work upon me. For ye have the poor always with you; but me ye have not always. For in that she hath poured this ointment on my body, she did it for my burial. Verily I say unto you, Wheresoever this gospel shall be preached in the whole world, there shall also this, that this woman hath done, be told for a memorial of her."

Acts 10:1-4,

"There was a certain man in Caesarea called Cornelius, a centurion of the band called the Italian band, A devout man, and one that feared God with all his house, which gave much alms to the people, and prayed to God alway. He saw in a vision evidently about the ninth hour of the day an angel of God coming in to him, and saying unto him, Cornelius. And when he looked on him, he was afraid, and said, What is it, Lord? And he said unto him, Thy prayers and thine alms are come up for a memorial before God."

17. Poverty is a spirit and is terminated with sacrificial seeds on the altar. Gideon broke down the altar of his father's house and terminated poverty in their family and their family being the least in Judges 6. Fire only comes down in response to sacrifices on altars. (1 Kings 18)

18. Priests must also bring a sacrifice. (Eli in 1 Samuel 1; Zacharias in Luke 1)

19. Solomon started his kingship with sacrifice and maintained his kingship by sacrifice. (1 Kings 3)

20. The power behind the altar you serve or give to, comes down to help you in your hour of need or trouble.

    Psalms 20:1-3,
    "The Lord hear thee in the day of trouble; the name of the God of Jacob defend thee; Send thee help from the sanctuary, and strengthen thee out of Zion; Remember all thy offerings, and accept thy burnt sacrifice; Selah."

21. Sacrifices Provoke God's voice, God's wisdom and God's intervention. (1 Kings 3; 5:1-3)

22. Sacrifices produce prosperity, provokes the prophetic from Angels for the termination of Barrenness. (Genesis 14; 18; 22)

23. Sacrifices Remove evil occurrences.

    Jeremiah 32:22
    "And hast given them this land, which thou didst swear to their fathers to give them, a land flowing with milk and honey;..."

Jeremiah 32:26-29,

"Then came the word of the Lord unto Jeremiah, saying, Behold, I am the Lord, the God of all flesh: is there any thing too hard for me? Therefore thus saith the Lord; Behold, I will give this city into the hand of the Chaldeans, and into the hand of Nebuchadrezzar king of Babylon, and he shall take it: And the Chaldeans, that fight against this city, shall come and set fire on this city, and burn it with the houses, upon whose roofs they have offered incense unto Baal, and poured out drink offerings unto other gods, to provoke me to anger."

24. National and Family Plagues Are Only Averted, Removed and Terminated By Sacrifices and Vows.

2 Samuel 24:24-25,

"And the king said unto Araunah, Nay; but I will surely buy it of thee at a price: neither will I offer burnt offerings unto the Lord my God of that which doth cost me nothing. So David bought the threshingfloor and the oxen for fifty shekels of silver. And David built there an altar unto the Lord, and offered burnt offerings and peace offerings. So the Lord was intreated for the land, and the plague was stayed from Israel."

A Sacrifice Is Not A Sacrifice Until It Costs You Something Costly! Nothing Of Value Comes Cheap Or Free! Sacrifices remove and terminate national plagues and barrenness.

25. Sacrifices change one's destiny. When Gideon broke down his father's altar, and erected a new altar unto God with a sacrifice, his destiny changed in Judges 6. Why Destroy your father's altar? Because, the demons responsible for Generational poverty and impoverishment came by sacrifice and it will take another and a higher sacrifice for them to leave. They will only leave by sacrifice.

The only act that could release Israel was sacrifice as instructed (Judges 6:25-33). After the sacrifice and blowing the trumpet, 32,000 men appeared which signifies your sacrifice brings members to your church as a Pastor.

Psalm 11:3,
"If the foundations be destroyed, what can the righteous do?"

2 Kings 3:26-27,
"And when the king of Moab saw that the battle was too sore for him, he took with him seven hundred men that drew swords, to break through even unto the king of Edom: but they could not. Then he took his eldest son that should have reigned in his stead, and offered him for a burnt offering upon the wall. And there was great indignation against Israel: and they departed from him, and returned to their own land."

It took a sacrifice to breakthrough.

UNDERSTANDING SACRIFICES:

God sacrificed Jesus to save and restore us back to Eden. (John 3:16) It took the sacrifice of Jesus to get him qualified to open the books and seals recorded in Revelation 5:2-5,

"And I saw a strong angel proclaiming with a loud voice, Who is worthy to open the book, and to loose the seals thereof? And no man in heaven, nor in earth, neither under the earth, was able to open the book, neither to look thereon. And I wept much, because no man was found worthy to open and to read the book, neither to look thereon. And one of the elders saith unto me, Weep not: behold, the Lion of the tribe of Juda, the Root of David, hath prevailed to open the book, and to loose the seven seals thereof."

It took a sacrifice to secure our healing and divine health. (1 Peter 2:24; Isaiah 53:4-5; Matthew 8:17) It took a sacrifice to secure our healing and divine prosperity. (2 Corinthians 8:9)

In 2 Samuel 24, it took a sacrifice to avert a national plague.

In Genesis 22, it took the sacrifice of Isaac to convince God of Abraham's love and to secure sworn blessings. In Genesis 27, Isaac requested 'Give me venison, such as I love...' It took the kind of venison Isaac loved to pronounce the generational patriarchal blessing on Jacob which translated him from an individual to a nation.

A SACRIFICE IS NOT A SACRIFICE UNTIL IT COSTS YOU SOMETHING! I Repeat: 'Sacrifice is not Sacrifice until it Costs you Something.'

New Testament Examples of Spiritual Sacrifices. (1 Peter 2:5-10)

We are a lively house called to offer spiritual sacrifice.

Revelation 1:6,
"And hath made us kings and priests unto God and his Father; to him be glory and dominion for ever and ever. Amen."

Revelation 5:10,
"You have made them to be a kingdom and priests to serve our God, and they will reign on the earth."

As Christians, we are priests and priests offer sacrifices and the kind of spiritual sacrifices that priests offer include:

a. Doing Good - Galatians 6:6,
    "Let him that is taught in the word communicate unto him that teacheth in all good things."

b. Offer of thanksgiving - Hebrews 13:15-16,
    "By him therefore let us offer the sacrifice of praise to God continually, that is, the fruit of our lips giving thanks to his name. But to do good and to communicate forget not: for with such sacrifices God is well pleased."

c.   Communicating – Giving, 1 Timothy 6:18,
"That they do good, that they be rich in good works, ready to distribute, willing to communicate"

THE POWER OF SACRIFICES

Sacrifices are:

i.   The key to the Supernatural Anointing.

ii.   The key to Power

iii.   The key to Divine Wisdom

iv.   The key to God's Presence

v.   The key to Divine Prosperity and Wealth

vi.   The key to Manifestation of signs, wonders and power

vii.   The key to Dramatic Turnarounds

viii. The key to Restoration and Restitution

ix.   What you need to do to change your situation

x.   The key to DOING SOMETHING YOU HAVE NEVER DONE TO ATTRACT, RECEIVE, HANDLE SOMETHING YOU HAVE NEVER ATTRACTED, RECEIVED OR HANDLED BEFORE.

So, do something you have never done before to receive what you have never had. If God can speak to a donkey, there is nothing else He cannot do. The question is, are you willing to pay the price?

The day you change your position/attitude, God will change your situation and altitude. A typical example is the thief on the cross beside Jesus, whose destination was changed instantly when he changed his attitude. (Luke 23:43) So, the question you must ask is, 'What will God have me do to become what God wants me to become?'

Every time you lift up your hand to God, you are offering Sacrifice, which God accepts just like a humble spirit because humility is a spiritual sacrifice. (Psalm 107:22; Psalm 141:2; Psalm 51:17) You ought to be living in and remain in the realm of sacrifices in order to remain a royal priesthood that God has made you through the blood of our Lord Jesus Christ. (Romans 12:1,2)

Every time we give to God or give on altars, we are offering a spiritual sacrifice. That's why we should never be fed up of giving offerings. (Philippians 4:15; Galatians 6: 9)

As we saw from the beginning, the definition of the word SACRIFICE from the Advance Learners Dictionary is: The giving up of something of great value to oneself for a special purpose or to benefit someone else.

God is a special purpose and so is Jesus and His kingdom. Sacrificing to do God's business could be in the form of money, time, talent, word, study time, prayer, soul winning, church attendance, follow up, etc. Whenever you stop or cut down on your outflow of giving offerings, you either stop or cut the inflow of blessing into your life. (Revelation 13)

EXAMPLES OF SACRIFICE:

Paul's first encounter with God on the road to Damascus in Acts 9, starts with, 'What will you have me do?' (First question). This is the key to significance, relevance, impact, influence, affluence, abundance, prosperity, wisdom. What am I here for? This is the secret to fulfilment in life.

Don't only come to church for a solution; BE THE SOLUTION!

BECOME AN ANSWER TO SOMEONE'S PRAYER ALWAYS!

YOU COULD BE A SOLUTION TO SOMEONE ELSE'S PROBLEM. YOU COULD BE THE ANSWER IF YOU COME TO CHURCH TO GIVE AND NOT JUST TO TAKE ALWAYS!!

Many have turned churches into 'Take-away' centres. Your sacrificial offering starting with your life as a seed, answers problems in church and in your society. Paul's testimony of the Macedonian church is worth emulating by us, who are the 21st century Christians.

2 Corinthians 8:1-7 reads:
"Moreover, brethren, we do you to wit of the grace of God bestowed on the churches of Macedonia; How that in a great trial of affliction the abundance of their joy and their deep poverty abounded unto the riches of their liberality. For to their power, I bear record, yea, and beyond their

power they were willing of themselves; Praying us with much intreaty that we would receive the gift, and take upon us the fellowship of the ministering to the saints. And this they did, not as we hoped, but first gave their own selves to the Lord, and unto us by the will of God. Insomuch that we desired Titus, that as he had begun, so he would also finish in you the same grace also. Therefore, as ye abound in every thing, in faith, and utterance, and knowledge, and in all diligence, and in your love to us, see that ye abound in this grace also."

Put down your pride and serve, help pack up in church, in the house of God. Your gift will make a way for you. Use your talent, gift, prayer, intercession, ministry of helps as a sacrifice, etc. Obeying God's command through God's servant such as Haggai 1:2-14 can result in you qualifying for Haggai 2:6-9. Give your Tithes and Offerings; Live holy lives. Sacrifice your flesh for supremacy of and for things of the Spirit.

Christians these days are more concerned about what they can get from church than what they can do for the church just like the disciples who said, 'We have left all; What do we get in return?'

Note Matthew 10:39
"HE THAT FINDETH HIS LIFE SHALL LOSE IT: AND HE THAT LOSETH HIS LIFE FOR MY SAKE SHALL FIND IT."

God has always been and especially in these last days is looking for men and women who will be willing and obedient to literally make some sacrifices and say with Isaiah in Isaiah 62:1-2, *"For Zion's sake will; I not hold my peace and for Jerusalem's sake until I see the glory of God in Jerusalem."*

People who will do anything, deny themselves of comfort for Zion's SAKE. Today, people don't pray and don't feel guilty, won't tithe and don't feel guilty, rebel and are worshipping God and chewing gum and texting at the same time saying in the house of the Lord, there is liberty.

Remember scripture says, 'Woe is he that sits at ease in Zion.' (Amos 6:1) and 'Woe unto anyone who does the work of God negligently.' (Jeremiah 48:10)

We need a holiness revival, a revival of whatever it takes to please God. We need a revival of the spirit of Daniel, Shadrach, Meshach, Abednego, Esther, Jeremiah, Nehemiah, Joshua, Paul, etc. Who will risk their lives to obey God. We need a revival of responsible people in the body of Christ again. We need a revival of people who will cry out to obey God. We can come to the point where we see the kind of miracles that old time revivals had.

Man will do everything to get material things and leave God's house to lie in waste, and yet the comforts will be used by these same members. This should be our prayer and attitude; for all of us to put God's house first.

- Some describe Europe, as Babylon because of perversion, carnality, total disregard for God and all forms of spirituality.

  Psalms 22:30,
  "A seed shall serve him; it shall be accounted to the Lord for a generation."

  John 12:24-25,
  "Verily, verily, I say unto you, Except a corn of wheat fall into the ground and die, it abideth alone: but if it die, it bringeth forth much fruit. He that loveth his life shall lose it; and he that hateth his life in this world shall keep it unto life eternal."

- Be willing to be a Daniel in Babylon; you can make a difference. Sacrifice your life.

- That's why, the Psalmist, the addicted lover of God said in Psalms 137:5-6,
  "If I forget thee, O Jerusalem, let my right hand forget her cunning. If I do not remember thee, let my tongue cleave to the roof of my mouth; if I prefer not Jerusalem above my chief joy."

That is, if I do not prefer God and his Kingdom far above my family, business, pleasures, etc., let my tongue cleave to the upper part of my mouth.

Members of churches sometimes wonder why Ministers have more anointing and look younger and stronger than they do. The answer is Sacrifice of time though working on a secular job, to pray, study and serve God in various capacities. It is the sacrifices they make. Remember what God has done for you so far and sacrifice your self on God's altar. (Genesis 22; 1 Timothy 4:15)

Our going to missions to preach without love offering and the usual comforts are all sacrifices. JESUS left his throne and exalted position, he offered himself as a living sacrifice just as we are exhorted by Paul in Romans 12:1,2 to do. He became poor that we through his poverty might become rich (2 Corinthians 8:9). That is what SACRIFICE is. We must lay our lives down for others to see them saved, delivered, blessed and set free, consolidated to become disciples. (John 1:12; Matthew 28:19-20)

Jesus LEFT HEAVEN TO COME ON EARTH TO DIE FOR US AND YET SOME CHRISTIANS CANNOT EVEN CROSS THE ROAD TO GO TO A CHURCH THAT IS OPPOSITE THEIR HOUSE! What A SHOCK!!!

OLD TESTAMENT EXAMPLES OF SACRIFICE:

i. Every time we make or give a sacrifice, the Holy Ghost comes down with fire to consume our sacrifice. (1 Kings 18; Acts 1:8; 2; 4:31)

ii. Fire only comes down at a response to sacrifice. No one ever got God to send fire upon an empty altar. FIRE ONLY COMES DOWN IN RESPONSE TO SACRIFICES ON ALTARS:

1 Kings 18:31-39,
"And Elijah took twelve stones, according to the number of the tribes of the sons of Jacob, unto whom the word of the Lord came, saying, Israel shall be thy name: And with the stones he built an altar in the name of the Lord: and he made a trench about the altar, as great as would contain two measures of seed. And he put the wood in order, and cut the bullock in pieces, and laid him on the wood, and said, Fill four barrels with water, and pour it on the burnt sacrifice, and on the wood. And he said, Do it the second time. And they did it the second time. And he said, Do it the third time. And they did it the third time. And the water ran round about the altar; and he filled the trench also with water. And it came to pass at the time of the offering of the evening sacrifice, that Elijah the prophet came near, and said, Lord God of Abraham, Isaac, and of Israel, let it be known this day that thou art God in Israel, and that I am thy servant, and that I have done all these things at thy word. Hear me, O Lord, hear me, that this people may know that thou art the Lord God, and that thou hast turned their heart back again. Then the fire of the Lord fell, and consumed the burnt sacrifice, and the wood, and the stones, and the dust, and licked up the water that was

in the trench. And when all the people saw it, they fell on their faces: and they said, The Lord, he is the God; the Lord, he is the God."

FIRE LICKED UP WATER: Normally Water Puts Out Fire But, Sacrifices Cause God To Use Fire To Lick or Swallow Water. That's the Power of Sacrifices on ALTARS!!

iii. Every time we make a sacrifice on God's altar, we smoke God out of heaven and receive heaven's signals like King Solomon did in 1 Kings 3. We get God's attention and hear His signals, intentions, voice and instructions including a request for what we desire. (Acts 13:1,2).

iv. Sacrifices cause God to set you on high above your contemporaries including giving your life as a seed and your sacrificial offerings. Jesus was more anointed without measure because he loved righteousness saying 'I must be about my father's business while it is day, for the night cometh when no one can work.'

Psalm 45:7,
"Thou lovest righteousness, and hatest wickedness: therefore God, thy God, hath anointed thee with the oil of gladness above thy fellows."

(John 9:4; 4:34; Deuteronomy 28:1-14)
You can't put God first and be last in life!! Impossible!!

v.   True and sincere love is expressed in what you give not what you get. (John 3:16, 2 Corinthians 8:5-8)

a. All Lovers Are Givers But Not All Givers Are Lovers.

Ask some men or women who they want to get married to and they say one who can do this or that for me, and this for me and that for me, etc. selfish love – no sacrifice.

b. Not all givers are lovers, but, all lovers are givers. John 3:16, *"For God so loved the world, that he gave his only begotten Son, that whosoever believeth in him should not perish, but have everlasting life."*

c. Love is demonstrated in giving.

d. The Proof of Love is in GIVING:

2 Corinthians 8:5, 8-9,

"And this they did, not as we hoped, but first gave their own selves to the Lord, and unto us by the will of God...I speak not by commandment, but by occasion of the forwardness of others, and to prove the sincerity of your love. For ye know the grace of our Lord Jesus Christ, that, though he was rich, yet for your sakes he became poor, that ye through his poverty might be rich."

1 Kings 3:3-5,

"And Solomon loved the Lord, walking in the statutes of David his father: only he sacrificed and

burnt incense in high places. And the king went to Gibeon to sacrifice there; for that was the great high place: a thousand burnt offerings did Solomon offer upon that altar.

In Gibeon the Lord appeared to Solomon in a dream by night: and God said, "Ask what I shall give thee."

Genesis 22:10-12,
"And Abraham stretched forth his hand, and took the knife to slay his son. And the angel of the Lord called unto him out of heaven, and said, Abraham, Abraham: and he said, Here am I. And he said, Lay not thine hand upon the lad, neither do thou any thing unto him: for now I know that thou fearest (LOVEST) God, seeing thou hast not withheld thy son, thine only son from me."

GIVING IS THE MOST AUTHENTIC AND MOST CREDIBLE PROOF OF LOVE!

vi. What you are called as a title in church or the Ministry does not matter, it's what you do with what you have to add value that matters. THERE IS NO ENTITLEMENT IN TITLES; THERE IS ONLY ENTITLEMENT IN ACCOMPLISHMENTS! God always loves and expects sacrifices.

vii. Don't sacrifice your future for the present; Sacrifice your present for your future i.e. sacrifice your energy, time and resources to work in the kingdom now. It's however, time that shows those who work hard. As the saying goes: It's only when the tide is out that you discover those who swam naked!

viii. If you don't stand for anything in particular, you will fall for everything in general.

ix. Jesus said, 'I must work while it is day, for the night cometh when no man can work.' If you are going to be hated for what you stand for and do for the Kingdom, be hated now. They will learn to understand and appreciate you and your stand when they see the tremendous results of your labour and sacrifice. After all, the servant is not greater than the Master. (John 15:20)

- Whatever you did yesterday is why you are where you are today.

- What you do today will determine where you will be tomorrow.

x. **Every great achievement comes through a present sacrifice.**

A Word of Advice for those who are not married: Don't let anyone pressurise you into marrying just anyone because if you marry just anyone, they will speak of you till Jesus comes. Don't eat an unripe fruit. Don't put your foot in an oversize shoe. Don't light certain fires before their time.

Song of Solomon 8:3,
"I charge you, O daughters of Jerusalem, that ye stir not up, nor awake my love, until he please."

Ecclesiastes 10:8,
"He that diggeth a pit shall fall into it; and whoso breaketh an hedge, a serpent shall bite him."

Wait! Isaiah 40:31 says,
"They that wait upon the Lord shall renew their strength; they shall mount up with wings like eagles, they shall run and not be weary and they shall walk and not faint."

[Order my books on relationships from www. houseofjudah.org.uk]

xi. Only fools sacrifice their future for their present.

Ecclesiastes 5:1,
"Keep thy foot when thou goest to the house of God, and be more ready to hear, than to give the sacrifice of fools: for they consider not that they do evil."

xii. Don't be in a hurry to leave God's house after church; do something beneficial and helpful; help someone, talk to someone, encourage someone, disciple someone, give to someone, ask what you can do, help tidy up before you leave; sacrifice your present for your future.

xiii. Pursue Wisdom and In All Your Getting, Get an Understanding of the Power of Sacrifices.

Proverbs 1:5,
"A wise man will hear, and will increase learning; and a man of understanding shall attain unto wise counsels:"

Proverbs 19:20-21,
"Hear counsel, and receive instruction, that thou mayest be wise in thy latter end. There are many devices (plans) in a man's heart; nevertheless (but only) the counsel of the Lord, that shall stand. (Shall prevail)"

Proverbs 2:6-7,
"For the Lord giveth wisdom: out of his mouth cometh knowledge and understanding. He layeth up sound wisdom for the righteous: he is a buckler to them that walk uprightly"

Proverbs 4:7-9,
"Wisdom is the principal thing; therefore get wisdom: and with all thy getting get understanding. Exalt her, and she shall promote thee: she shall bring thee to honour, when thou dost embrace her. She shall give to thine head an ornament of grace: a crown of glory shall she deliver to thee."

Proverbs 17:27,
"He that hath knowledge spareth his words: and a man of understanding is of an excellent spirit."

Excellence is the answer to racism and sexism.
Receive understanding now. NOTE: For those who come to
church on Sundays only, read this:

> Proverbs 21:16,
> *"The man that wandereth out of the way of*
> *understanding shall remain in the congregation of the*
> *dead."*

xiv. Sacrifice cancels or exchanges physical things for
Spiritual things.

xv. Sacrifices avert national plagues.

> 2 Samuel 24:24-25,
> *"And the king said unto Araunah, Nay; but I will*
> *surely buy it of thee at a price: neither will I offer burnt*
> *offerings unto the Lord my God of that which doth cost*
> *me nothing. So David bought the threshingfloor and*
> *the oxen for fifty shekels of silver. And David built there*
> *an altar unto the Lord, and offered burnt offerings and*
> *peace offerings. So the Lord was intreated for the land,*
> *and the plague was stayed from Israel."*

xvi. Sacrifices that cost you something, terminates God's
fury and appeases God to command the Angel of Death
to withdraw their sword from committing genocide.

1 Chronicles 21:24-28,

"And king David said to Ornan, Nay; but I will verily buy it for the full price: for I will not take that which is thine for the Lord, nor offer burnt offerings without cost. So David gave to Ornan for the place six hundred shekels of gold by weight. And David built there an altar unto the Lord, and offered burnt offerings and peace offerings, and called upon the Lord; and he answered him from heaven by fire upon the altar of burnt offering. And the Lord commanded the angel; and he put up his sword again into the sheath thereof. At that time when David saw that the Lord had answered him in the threshingfloor of Ornan the Jebusite, then he sacrificed there."

xvii. Sacrifices give you power to get wealth and brings you so much wealth to prepare for the next generation to build God a house.

1 Chronicles 22:5,

"And David said, Solomon my son is young and tender, and the house that is to be builded for the Lord must be exceeding magnifical, of fame and of glory throughout all countries: I will therefore now make preparation for it. So David prepared abundantly before his death."

1 Chronicles 29:1-5,

"Furthermore David the king said unto all the congregation, Solomon my son, whom alone God hath chosen, is yet young and tender, and the work is great:

for the palace is not for man, but for the Lord God. Now I have prepared with all my might for the house of my God the gold for things to be made of gold, and the silver for things of silver, and the brass for things of brass, the iron for things of iron, and wood for things of wood; onyx stones, and stones to be set, glistering stones, and of divers colours, and all manner of precious stones, and marble stones in abundance. Moreover, because I have set my affection to the house of my God, I have of mine own proper good, of gold and silver, which I have given to the house of my God, over and above all that I have prepared for the holy house, Even three thousand talents of gold, of the gold of Ophir, and seven thousand talents of refined silver, to overlay the walls of the houses withal: The gold for things of gold, and the silver for things of silver, and for all manner of work to be made by the hands of artificers. And who then is willing to consecrate his service this day unto the Lord?"

Don't sacrifice your God for money, but sacrifice your money for God.

Note: When you don't pray in the morning because you're too busy, that will be the day when the devil will be too busy on you.

GIFTS AND SACRIFICES MAKE ROOM FOR YOU AND BRING YOU BEFORE GREAT MEN.

Examples:

A. In 1 Kings 18, before fire came down, Elijah had to offer sacrifices.

B. Samson's parents offered sacrifices first and Bible says, '...the Angel did wondrously.'

Judges 13:19 (KJV),
"So Manoah took a kid with a meat offering, and offered it upon a rock unto the LORD: and the angel did wondrously; and Manoah and his wife looked on."

Judges 13:19 NIV,
"Then Manoah took a young goat, together with the grain offering, and sacrificed it on a rock to the LORD. And the LORD did an amazing thing while Manoah and his wife watched."

Nothing meaningful and lasting ever happens without sacrifices. Fire Only Comes down in response to a sacrifice.

C. God had respect unto Abel's sacrifice because of his sacrificial offering of the first fruits and fat thereof. (Genesis 4)

D. Psalm 126:5,6 says,

   "They that sow in tears shall reap in joy. He that goeth forth and weeping (offering) bearing precious seed shall doubtless come again with rejoicing, bringing his sheaves with him."

E. Unto none was Elijah sent but unto the Widow of Zarephath. The Instruction was: MAKE ME FIRST: The widow had to make Elijah, the prophet, a meal first before she and her son ate any, then and only then was shortage, lack, insufficiency and poverty eliminated from her life permanently.

   1 Kings 17:13,
   "And Elijah said unto her, Fear not; go and do as thou hast said: but make me thereof a little cake first, and bring it unto me, and after make for thee and for thy son."

   Her Latter End Became Far Better Than Her Beginning:
   1 Kings 17:15-16,
   "And she went and did according to the saying of Elijah: and she, and he, and her house, did eat many days. And the barrel of meal wasted not, neither did the cruse of oil fail, according to the word of the Lord, which he spake by Elijah."

   Prophets are usually sent to take offerings from you for a prophetic purpose. e.g. you make a room for them and when they lie and wake up, you become pregnant as we saw clearly in 2 Kings 4.

F. It is the meeting you did not feel like coming to or the money you did not want to give or the all-night prayer meeting you did not want to attend that counts more with God. Remember, Paul and Silas in Acts 19 - The Macedonia experience.

Sacrifice Is Not Sacrifice Until It Costs You Something!!

G. God wanted Isaac offered as a sacrifice in Genesis 22. Why didn't God bless him, i.e. Abraham before the sacrifice or make such pronouncement. It was only after he offered Isaac that God pronounced irrevocable blessing saying "...in blessing will I bless thee, in multiplying will I multiply thee as the stars in the sky and as the sand on the seashore..."

H. In Genesis 27, It was only after Isaac, the father and patriarch's venison (his favourite stew) had been made and brought to Him by Jacob, that, he pronounced the blessing on Jacob! By overlooking the fact that Jacob was not the hairy one (notice the obvious difference in asking for prayer from your pastor with a gift).

I. Bible testifies: 'ONLY HE, Solomon in 1 Kings 3:3 - He loved God', offered sacrifices, a 1000 burnt offering that smoked God out of heaven to appear to him in a vision and asked him what he wanted him to do for him. If you really want to see visions, offer sacrifices.

These questions are very important and being repeated for very obvious reasons:

Why did God not appear to Solomon until he offered sacrifices? Because, Proverbs 18:16 says, 'A man's gift maketh room for him and brings him before great men.'

When you make sacrifices, God will ask you **'what do you want?'** Not before. Understand that it's only after you've offered sacrifices that God makes certain generational pronouncements. So, develop a lifestyle of giving your tithes and offerings consistently and making sacrifices to help others especially God's work i.e. KINGDOM BUSINESS. (Galatians 6:6-10; 2 Corinthians 9:6-9)

Your gift, your sacrifices will make room for you and bring you before the great to learn from them the secrets/keys that made them great so you also become great or greater.

J. The woman with alabaster ointment - costly alabaster ointment. She was in the same room with Jesus, his disciples and the guests but no one took notice of her until the moment she offered this ointment/perfume as a sacrifice [this ointment she sacrificed to wash Jesus' feet was equivalent to a whole years labourer's wages] and washed Jesus' feet. As a result of this sacrificial giving/ offering, her name was to be mentioned as a memorial anywhere the gospel was preached till date placing this act in the same category as Communion. (Mark 14)

K.   Joseph of Arimathaea in Luke 23:50-56. Before now, he had not been heard of but as a result of his shameless sacrificial act of boldly showing up to claim Jesus' body and burying him among the rich in his tomb, his name becomes known and his town, which before now was unknown to many.

SACRIFICIAL OFFERINGS have the inherent power and tendency to BECOME MEMORIALS IN GOD'S SIGHT.

Scripture says, Greater love hath no man than this that a man should lay down his life for his friends, as a SACRIFICE.

Always Be Willing To Communicate:
Philippians 4:15,
"Now ye Philippians know also, that in the beginning of the gospel, when I departed from Macedonia, no church communicated with me as concerning giving and receiving, but ye only."

Only those who communicate (give to support or partner with God's servants, churches and ministries) qualify for Philippians 4:19.

Philippians 4:15-19.

"Now ye Philippians know also, that in the beginning of the gospel, when I departed from Macedonia, no church communicated with me as concerning giving and receiving, but ye only. For even in Thessalonica ye sent once and again unto my necessity. Not because I desire a gift: but I desire fruit that may abound to your account. But I have all, and abound: I am full, having received of Epaphroditus the things which were sent from you, an odour of a sweet smell, a sacrifice acceptable, wellpleasing to God. But my God shall supply all your need according to his riches in glory by Christ Jesus."

Anyone who quotes Philippians 4:19 without doing Philippians 4:15 is a '419'. No Philippians '415', No Philippians '419'.

God is looking for those who will disrespect the god of money for Him. Does your riches have you? Anything you find difficult to give away, that thing has you, just like the rich young ruler.

*Fire Only Comes Down In
Response To Sacrifices!!*

Conclusion

WHAT TO DO!

- CATCH THIS, ACT ON THIS:
  Stop giving to men and start giving to God, i.e. when you are giving to men or church, remember you are giving to God and He is the Rewarder not men. (Hebrews 11:6)
  Respect Altars!

- **Give God a special sacrificial offering and He will CAUSE MEN (By Revelation), FORCE MEN, IMPRESS ON MEN, INCONVENIENCE MEN, COMPEL MEN (ANAGKAZO, BIAZO, ANAIDEIA) TO GIVE TO YOU. (Luke 6:38)**

- A pastor who did not give much offering had to sow N4000 got N25,000 x 5 + N10, 000 etc + healing.

- Write down 7 things you would like God to cause men to give to you whether they like it or not.

- Give your man of God an offering and the anointing will come upon him like Elijah to ask, 'What does she/he need? Remember, Elijah and Elisha asked their servants what the people needed after they had blessed them or giving to them.

- VITAL TRUTHS TO ACT ON

- **Remember: What Faith Cannot Do, Faithfulness Will Do.**

God said: DO WHAT YOU MUST DO AND I WILL DO WHAT I MUST DO:

Psalm 50:5-6,
"Gather my saints together unto me; those that have made a covenant with me by sacrifice. And the heavens shall declare his righteousness: for God is judge himself. Selah."

Psalms 50:7-15,
"Hear, O my people, and I will speak; O Israel, and I will testify against thee: I am God, even thy God. I will not reprove thee for thy sacrifices or thy burnt offerings, to have been continually before me. I will take no bullock out of thy house, nor he goats out of thy folds. For every beast of the forest is mine, and the cattle upon a thousand hills. I know all the fowls of the mountains: and the wild beasts of the field are mine. If I were hungry, I would not tell thee: for the world is mine, and the fulness thereof. Will I eat the flesh of bulls, or drink the blood of goats? Offer unto God thanksgiving; and pay thy vows unto the

most High: And call upon me in the day of trouble: I will deliver thee, and thou shalt glorify me."

As a result of Abraham's offering of Isaac in Genesis 22, he got Jesus and us.

- **Do what you have never done before to get what you have never received before.**

- **Give Convenient and Inconvenient offerings. Anointing brings productivity.**

- **Sacrifice what you have now to get what you need tomorrow.**

- Thus saith the LORD, 'ZERO IN ON WHAT YOU WANT' (Luke 6:38).

- 'Stop giving to men and stop saying, 'men will not give me this or that...'

- 'Give unto me and I will cause men to give to you...'

- **'Do something you've never done before and God will give you what you have never received before'.**

2 Chronicles 20:20b says,
"...believe in God and you shall be established, believe his prophets and you shall prosper."
Psalm 126,

'Sow in tears, prayer, your money, your time and you shall reap in joy.'

This is the secret behind how I became who I am now; value those who are over you in the Lord. (Ephesians 6:1-3)

Some of you are not experiencing the breakthroughs you need to experience because you are not taking good care of your pastors:

Hebrews 7:7
"Forget not the Levites, irrespective of whether they are prospering, working or not. Remember: 'Without contradiction, the lesser is blessed by the greater."

When Was The Last Time You Blessed Your Pastor Financially?

Remember: SACRIFICIAL OFFERINGS have the inherent power and tendency to BECOME MEMORIALS IN GOD'S SIGHT!

Deuteronomy 14:27-29, New Century Version (NCV)
"Do not forget the Levites in your town, because they have no land of their own among you. At the end of every third year, everyone should bring one-tenth of that year's crop and store it in your towns. This is for the Levites so they may eat and be full. (They have no land of their own among you.) It is also for strangers, orphans, and widows who live in your towns so that all

of them may eat and be full. Then the Lord your God will bless you and all the work you do."

Start Now!

Do what you've never done before to experience what you've never experienced before!

AS we close this chapter, Let me show you HOW TO TRIGGER A GENERATIONAL AND IRREVERSIBLE BLESSING FROM OUR ALTAR:

DONATE ONLINE: Log on to our website www. houseofjudah.org.uk and SOW A SACRIFICIAL SEED OR BECOME A VISION PARTNER online TO TRIGGER WHAT YOUR HANDS HAVE NEVER HANDLED BEFORE.

I decree that as you do this faithfully and joyfully with great expectation, my God, the God who called me from the beginning and has never failed me, not once, will catapult you into scaling higher heights in your field in Jesus mighty name. You shall break forth to the right, left, centre, north, south, east and west in Jesus mighty name.

Let me hear from you by sending me an email at:
michaelhuttonwood@gmail.co
bishopmhw@gmail.com

You can join our covenant partners online at:
michaelhutton-wood.org
www.houseofjudah.org.uk

LIVE IN THE REALM
OF OFFERING SACRIFICES.

The Greatest Gift

If you want to take advantage of the contents of this message by asking God to give you power to lead, from which Adam fell, you need to give your life to Jesus Christ. If you have never met or experienced a definite encounter with Jesus Christ, you can know Him today. You can make your life right with Him by accepting Him as your personal Lord and Saviour by praying the following prayer out loud where you are. Pray this prayer with me now.

> **PRAYER FOR SALVATION:**
> "O God, I ask you to forgive me for my sins. I believe You sent Jesus to die on the cross for me and confess it with my mouth. I receive Jesus Christ as my personal Lord and Saviour and confess Him as Lord of my life and I give my life willingly to Him now. Thank you Lord for saving me and for making me a new person in Jesus' Name, (2 Corinthians 5:17) Amen."

If you prayed this prayer, you have now become a child of God (John 1:12) and I welcome you to the family of God. Please let me know about your decision for Jesus by writing to me. I would like to send you some free literature to help you in your new walk with the Lord.

So send me an email:
info@houseofjudah.org.uk
michaelhuttonwood@gmail.com

Or Call (within the UK):
0208 689 6010 / 07956 815 714

Outside the UK:
+44 208 689 6010 / +44 7956 815 714

Or visit us at:
www.houseofjudah.org.uk
michaelhutton-wood.org

Other Books & Leadership Manuals By Author

1. A Must For Every New Convert
2. You Need To Do The Ridiculous In Order To Experience The Miraculous
3. 175 Reasons Why You Cannot And Will Not Fail In Life
4. What To Do In The Darkest Hour Of Your Trial [125 Bible Truths You Must Know, Believe, Remember, Confess And Do]
5. Why You Should Pray And How You Should Pray For Your Pastor And Your Church Daily
6. 200 Questions You Must Ask, Investigate And Know Before You Say 'I Do'
7. I Shall Rise Again
8. How To Negotiate Your Desired Future With Today's Currency
9. Leadership Secrets
10. Leadership Nuggets
11. Leadership Capsules
12. What Is Ministry?
13. Generating Finances For Ministry [Without Sweating, Begging, Toiling, Gimmicks]
14. Taking The Struggle Out Of Ministry
15. 101 Tips For A Great Marriage
16. What Husbands Want And What Wives 'Really' Want
17. My Daily Bible Reading Guide
18. Leaders Are Not Born; Leaders Are Raised
19. No Ringy, No Dingy
20. My Daily Bible Reading Guide
21. You Have Only One Life; Make It Count (New)
22. Success Has No Uncles (New)

Training Manuals For Impactful Leadership & Effective Ministry

- ACADEMY 101 [HOUSE OF JUDAH ACADEMY CURRICULUM]
- MINISTRY 101
- LEADERSHIP 101
- PASTORAL LEADERSHIP 101 from SCHOOL OF IMPACTFUL PASTORAL LEADERSHIP

To order copies of any of these books, ministry or leadership manuals or for a product catalog of other literature, and CDs, DVDs, write to:

Michael Hutton-Wood Ministries
1st Floor, 387 London Road, Croydon. CR0 3PB.
UK.

or [in the UK call] - 0208 689 6010;
   [outside UK call] + 44 208 6896010

You can also place your order online as you visit our website: www.houseofjudah.org.uk

You can also email us at:
Email: info@houseofjudah.org.uk
michaelhuttonwood@gmail.com

Global Initiatives and Ministries Within The Ministry

TV MINISTRY IN THE UK –

Watch Leadership Secrets on:

KICC TV SKY Channel 591

Tuesday – 3.00pm

Saturday – 5.30pm

Watch Us On:

- YouTube

- www.houseofjudah.org.uk

Partnering With A Global Ministry Within A Ministry

Michael Hutton-Wood Ministries (The HUTTONWOOD WORLD OUTREACH MINISTRY) is the apostolic, missions, world outreach, and evangelistic wing of the House of Judah (Praise) Ministries with a mission to God's end time church and the nations of the earth.

This ministry was born out of a strong God-given mandate to reach, touch and impact the nations of the earth with the gospel of Christ and bring back divine order, discipline, integrity, godly character, excellence and stability to God's people and God's house. It has a strong apostolic mandate to set in order the things that are out of order and lacking in the church [The Body of Christ] – (Titus 1:5).

Its mission is to save the lost at any cost, depopulate hell and populate heaven with souls that have experienced in full, the new birth, renewal of mind, to produce believers walking in the fullness of their Godly inheritance, divine health, prosperity and authority to take their homes, communities, cities and nations for Christ and occupy till Christ returns. It is to raise a people without spot, wrinkle or blemish. The man of God's passion and drive is that as truly as he lives, this earth shall be filled with the knowledge of the glory of the Lord as the waters cover the sea.

His determination is not to rest, hold back or keep silent until he sees the body of Christ established as a praise in the earth. (Numbers 14:21; Habakkuk 2:14; Isaiah 62:6-7)

If you would like to join the faithful brethren and partners of this great ministry by becoming a partner as we believe God for ten thousand partners to partner with this vision prayerfully and financially, ask for a copy of the partners' club commitment card by writing to:

Michael Hutton-Wood Ministries
[Hutton-Wood World Outreach]
1st Floor, 387 London Road, Croydon.
CR0 3PB.UK.

Alternatively, you can send a monthly contribution by cheque payable to our ministry or donate online at:

www.houseofjudah.org.uk

Call: +44 [0] 208 689 6010 for more details.

Philippians 4:19 be your portion and experience as you partner with this work and global mandate. Shalom!

Generational Leadership Training Institute [The Leaders' Factory]

The Mandate:

Raising Generational Leaders, Impacting Nations.

The Generational Leadership Training Institute (GLTI) is the Leadership training and mentoring wing of our ministry with a global mandate to raise leaders with a generational thinking mindset, not a now mentality and to fulfil the Law of Explosive Growth – To add growth, lead followers – To multiply, lead leaders.

This is a Bible College, Leadership Training Institute fulfilling the Matthew 9:37-38 mandate of developing and releasing labourers for the end time harvest. We offer fulltime and part time certificate, diploma, degree and short twelve-week courses in biblical studies, counselling, leadership, practical ministry and schools of prosperity. Its aim is to raise leaders who know and live not just by the anointing but by ministerial ethics, leaders who build with a long term mentality, who live today with tomorrow in mind.

The mission of this unique educational and impartation institution is to transform followers into generational leaders and its motto is to raise leaders of discipline, integrity, godly character and excellence - D.I.C.E.

For correspondence, full time, part time, online courses, prospectus, fees and registration forms for the next course:

Call:

0208 689 6010

Or write to:

The Registrar, GLTI, 1st Floor, 387 London Road, Croydon. CR0 3PB. UK or from outside UK call +44 208 689 6010.

Additional information can be obtained
from visiting our website:

www.houseofjudah.org.uk
(Look for THE LEADERS FACTORY)

This is a hutton-wood publication

Leaders Factory International

The Mandate:
'In the business of training, developing and raising and releasing more leaders and leaders of leaders.'

> *'Leaders must be close enough to relate to others, but far enough ahead to motivate them.'* – John Maxwell

> *'You must live with people to know their problems, and live with God in order to solve them.'* – P. T. Forsyth

If you, your organisation, college, university, business or church would like to invite Dr. Michael Hutton-Wood for a Motivational-speaking, mentoring or leadership coaching engagement or to organize or hold a Leaders Factory seminar or conference, Leadership Development or Human Capital building seminar, Emerging leaders seminar, Management seminar, Business seminar, Effective people-management, Wealth-creation seminar or training for your workers, leaders, staff, ministers, employers, employees, congregation, youth, etc. you can contact us on:

0208 689 6010 [UK]

+44208 689 6010 [OUTSIDE UK]

Alternatively by email at:

- info@houseofjudah.org.uk

- michaelhuttonwood@gmail.com

or leadersfactoryinternational@yahoo.com

Visit our websites:

www.houseofjudah.org.uk

michaelhutton-wood.org

Follow Bishop on:

Twitter, WhatsApp, Facebook, Instagram, YouTube, etc

MANDATE:

Releasing Potential - Maximizing Destiny

Raising Generational Leaders - Impacting Nations

SIMPA
(Sceptre International Ministers & Pastors Association)

This covenant mandate comes from Genesis 49:10:

'The sceptre [of Leadership] shall not depart from JUDAH, nor a lawgiver from between his feet, until Shiloh come and unto Him shall the gathering of the people be"

Other covenant scriptures backing this mandate are: Isaiah 55:4 & Titus 1:5. We have a leadership assignment to RAISE GENERATIONAL LEADERS TO IMPACT NATIONS BY DISCOVERING MEN/WOMEN AND EMPOWERING THEM TO RELEASE THEIR POTENTIAL TO MAXIMIZE THEIR DESTINY.

SIMPA is a multi-cultural fellowship/network of diverse Christian leaders, pastors and ministers that recognize the need for fathering, covering and mentoring. The heartbeat of the man of God is to pour into the willing and obedient what has made him and keeps making him from what he's learnt from his father in the Lord, his teachers and mentors which is working for him and producing maximally. He said: 'I discovered this secret early: Not to learn from or follow those who make promises but from those who have obtained the promises, proofs and results.' REMEMBER: YOU DON'T NEED TO MAKE NOISE TO MAKE NEWS. SO FOLLOW NEWS-MAKERS NOT NOISE-MAKERS!

These are a few of the mindsets of the man of God:
- When the students are ready, the teacher will teach.
- 'YOU NEED FATHERS TO FATHER YOU TO GROW FEATHERS TO FLY.' – Bishop Oyedepo
- 'Without a father to father you, you can never grow feathers to fly and go further in life, than they went and accomplish more than they did.' – Michael Hutton-Wood
- Don't raise money; raise men and you'll have all the money you need to accomplish your assignment.
- There is no new thing under the sun – King Solomon
- What you desire to attain, become and accomplish in life, someone has accomplished it – find them, follow them, learn from them, sow into them and their resource materials and you will do more than they did and get there faster.
- Teachers, Trainers, Mentors and Fathers give you speed/ acceleration in every field of endeavour.
- Isaac Newton is known to have said the following:
- 'If I have seen further it has been by standing on the shoulders of those who have gone ahead of me.'
- Variant translations: 'Plato is my friend, Aristotle is my friend, but my best friend is truth.'
- 'Plato is my friend — Aristotle is my friend — truth is a greater friend.'

- 'If I have seen further it is only by standing on the shoulders of giants.'
- Without a reference you can never become a reference.
- If you don't refer to anyone no one will refer to you.
- Who laid / lays hands on you and what did / do they leave behind?
- This is not a money-making venture but rather about covering and empowerment for fulfilment of destiny and assignment within time allocated.
- The goal of SIMPA is to spiritually cover, strengthen, equip, empower, train, mentor and encourage and lift up the arms/hands of both emerging and active [full and part time] pastors, ministers and leaders and by so doing release them to fulfil their respective assignments both in ministry and the market place.

If You Would Like To Be A Part of SIMPA, ask for a registration form & pamphlet from our information desk in House of Judah

Or email:
info@houseofjudah.org.uk
michaelhuttonwood@gmail.com

Or call [in the UK]: 0208 689 6010
[outside UK call]: +44 208 689 6010
requesting for SIMPA registration form and pamphlet.

– SEE YOU ON TOP!
 Shalom!
– Bishop

Partnership

In the UK write or send cheque donations to:

Michael Hutton-Wood Ministries

1st Floor, 387 London Road, Croydon. CR0 3PB

In the UK Call: 0208 689 6010; 07956 815 714

Outside the UK Call: +44 208 689 6010; + 44 7956 815 714

Fax: +44 20 8689 3301

Email:

info@houseofjudah.org.uk

michaelhuttonwood@gmail.com

leadersfactoryinternational@yahoo.com

Or visit or donate online at our secure WEBSITE:

www.houseofjudah.org.uk

hwp

Dr. Michael Hutton-Wood

© 2017

Notes

....
....
....
....
....
....
....
....
....
....
....
....
....
....
....
....
....

Notes